Durham
A PICTORIAL HISTORY

Framed by the lush tobacco of the 1970's, the first Duke tobacco factory.

Photograph by Frank A. Kostyu

At the foot of Church Street stood Union Station, much busier than this picture postcard suggests. The 65-foot tower was a Durham landmark from 1904 until the removal of the building in 1967. The station was built for the Southern, Norfolk and Western and the Seaboard Air Line Railroads by the John P. Pettijohn Company of Lynchburg, Virginia. The architects were the Milburn and Heister Company of Washington, D.C.

Postcard courtesy of Wyatt T. Dixon.

A PICTORIAL HISTORY

Durham

By Joel A. Kostyu & Frank A. Kostyu

Design by Fischbach & Edenton

Donning

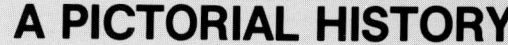

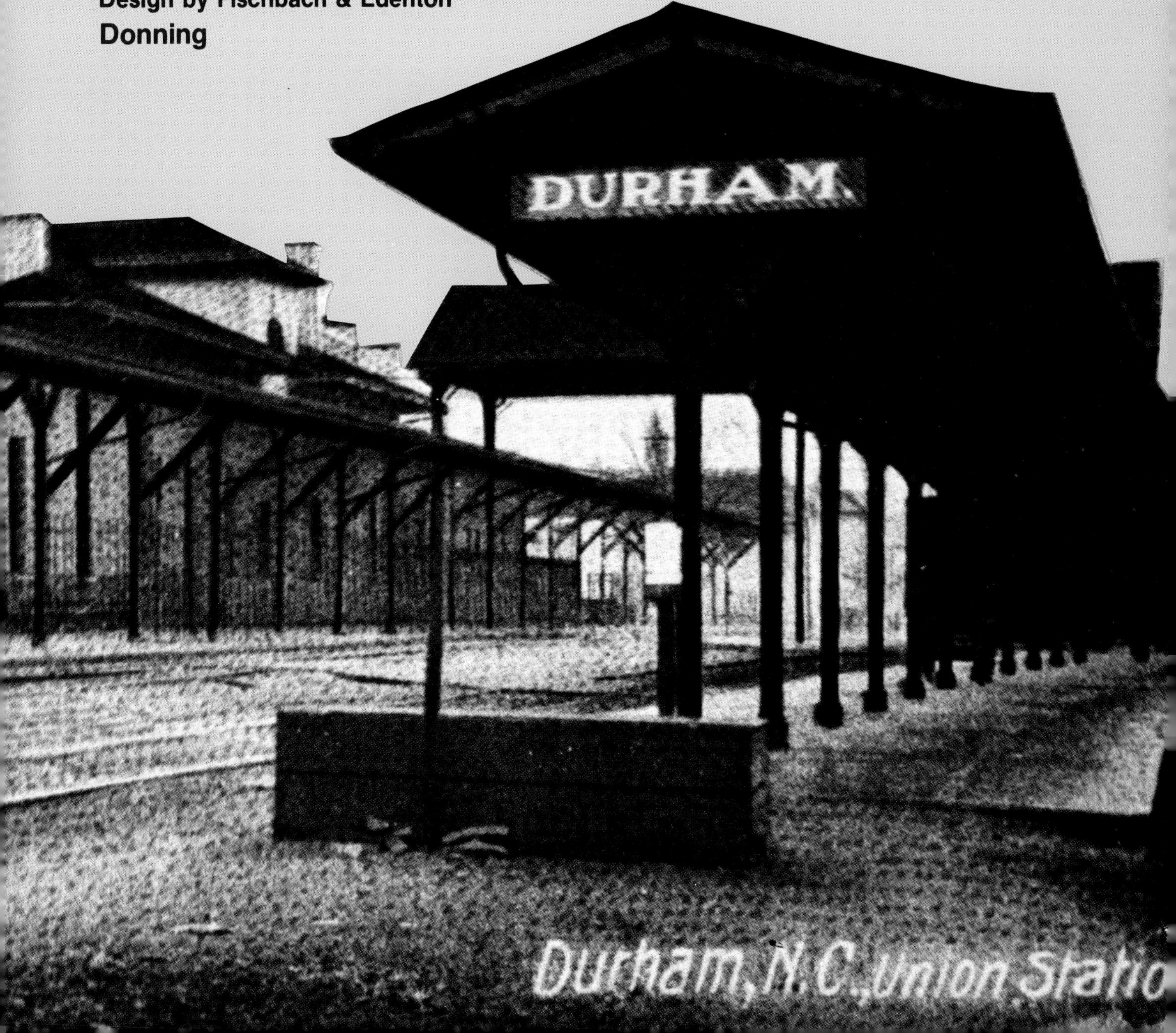
DURHAM.
Durham, N.C., Union Statio

This busy 1920s street scene shows Five Points, now known as Muirhead Plaza.

Photograph courtesy of Wyatt T. Dixon

Copyright© 1978 by Joel A. Kostyu and Frank A. Kostyu

All rights reserved, including the right to reproduce this book in any form whatsoever without permission in writing from the publisher, except for brief passages in connection with a review. For information, write: The Donning Company/ Publishers, 253 West Bute Street, Norfolk, Virginia 23510.

Library of Congress Cataloging in Publication Data:

Kostyu, Joel A., 1946-
Durham, a pictorial history.
SUMMARY: More than 350 pictures illustrate the history of this North Carolina city and its character today.
1. Durham, N.C.—History—Pictorial works.
2. Durham, N.C.—Description—Views. [1. Durham, N.C.—Pictorial works] I. Kostyu, Frank A., joint author. II. Title.
F264.D9K67   975.6'563   78-7817
ISBN 0-915442-48-5

Printed in the United States of America

Dedicated to the Citizens of Durham

CONTENTS

Introduction: The Early Years	8
By Wyatt T. Dixon	
Beginnings	18
Heritage Preserved	19
The Civil War	27
Reminiscences of a Durham Childhood:	36
The Turn of the Century	
By Elsie Wallace Perkins	
Industry & Commerce	46
Transportation	80
Education	89
People: The Lifeblood of Durham	112
Durham's Houses	129
Houses of Worship	138
Communication & Entertainment	151
Fashion	160
All Around the Town	167
Skylines	202
Acknowledgments	208

Photograph courtesy of the North Carolina Collection, Wilson Library, University of North Carolina, Chapel Hill

"The merit belongs to the beginner should his successor do even better."

Bartlett Snipes Durham was born in 1822 in the southern part of Orange County, some eight miles southwest of Chapel Hill. His parents were William and Polly Snipes Durham.

Even at an early age, Bartlett leaned toward becoming a doctor. As was the custom of the day, he took some training in the office of a physician relative and then went to Philadelphia for formal study before returning to the community that eventually took his name. Dr. Durham donated land to the North Carolina Railroad which, in appreciation, named its station Durham. The depot was established in 1850.

Dr. Durham's home, on what became the southeast corner of Corcoran Street near Main, was known as Pandora's Box. Here he lived as a bachelor, respected physician owning few worldly possessions. During the winter of 1858, he contracted pneumonia and died at the home of Dora White. Dr. Durham's body lay in state in the Eagle Hotel in Chapel Hill and then was taken to Antioch Church for the funeral service. He was buried in the Snipes family plot.

This painting of Dr. Bartlett Snipes Durham, from an original miniature, was completed in 1925 by Peter Phillips of New York City and is now owned by the Historic Preservation Society of Durham and on loan to the City Hall.

W. F. Carr, a councilman and former mayor of Durham, relates that he had heard that Dr. Durham was buried in a metal casket, with his gold-rimmed spectacles in place. With these facts in hand, efforts were made, some 70 years after Dr. Durham's death, to find the casket, exhume it, and prepare it for reburial. "We decided," wrote Carr in "The Durham Centennial Booklet," 1953, "to hire some hands with crowbars to comb Antioch Cemetery.... For days this crew worked in vain. Then, late one afternoon one of the hands struck a hard substance and the crowbar made a shining streak against an object. The casket was dug up and removed from the earth. At one end was a slide over glass. Breathlessly, we pushed back the slide and there to our wondering eyes appeared the gold-rimmed spectacles." The casket was taken to the Hall-Wynne Funeral Home and later re-interred in Maplewood Cemetery on January 1, 1934, as shown in this rare photograph.

Photograph courtesy of Wyatt T. Dixon

INTRODUCTION:

THE EARLY YEARS
By Wyatt T. Dixon

Wyatt T. Dixon is a Durham native and one of the foremost authorities on Durham history. He has written a weekly column on Durham's history for the Durham Sun *for over 40 years. Only semi-retired at age 83, Mr. Dixon has moved to a small home in the country, where he continues to write his column.*

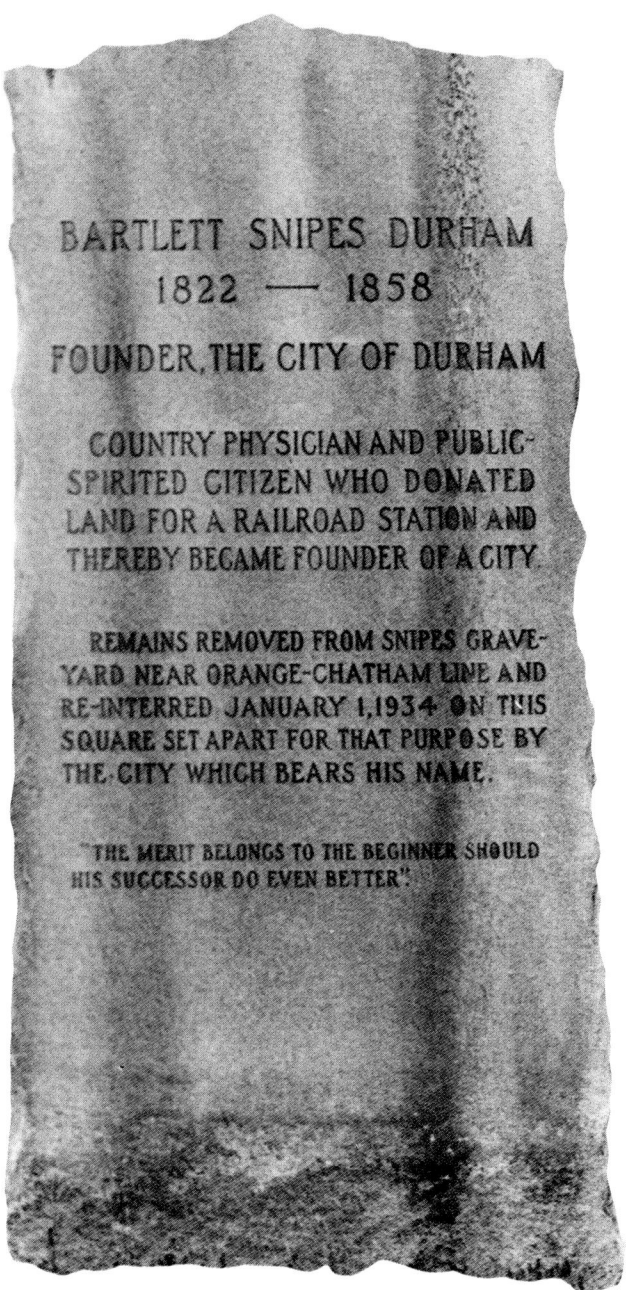

Entering the front gate of Annex B. of Maplewood Cemetery, the visitor will note on the left a well-kept, grassy knoll crowned by a huge memorial stone. The inscription reads:

BARTLETT SNIPES DURHAM

1822—1858

FOUNDER, THE CITY OF DURHAM

This memorial, surrounded by pine and flowering crab apple trees, was erected by the grateful people of Durham to mark the site of the final resting place of one of her most illustrious citizens and founder.

Photograph by Frank A. Kostyu

Durham is a comparatively new city. The time of its founding has never been definitely established, and exact information on its beginning died with the pioneers who settled here. Some even claim Durham was born by chance.

Durham might never have been founded but for the generosity of Dr. Bartlett Snipes Durham and the closefistedness of William Pratt. Pratt operated a large store in what is now the Ramseur Street area, a little community known as Prattsburg. Fearful that passing trains might frighten the horses of his customers, with a resulting loss of his business, he declined to grant the North Carolina Railroad, then gradually extending its tracks westward, land for a depot. Dr. Durham, seeing the great potential of a station, immediately offered a tract of four acres, which was accepted by the railroad. In recognition of the gift, the railroad named the new settlement for him.

Boyd's history, published in 1925, indicates the location of a post office as early as 1850, while Paul's history, written in 1884, states that Durham was established in 1852. When thought was directed to the founding year by local citizens who conceived the idea of celebrating its beginning, considerable research resulted. The United States Postal Service Department reported the establishment of a post office here on April 26, 1853. Since this was regarded as official and undisputed information, a research committee named by the Chamber of Commerce adopted that date as the official birthday of the town.

The town was incorporated April 10, 1869, through the passage of a bill introduced in the legislature by T. M. Argo. Durham had previously been incorporated, but, due to an 1867 act of Congress, no valid government existed in any Southern state. The approval by the state legislature of a second charter was thus necessary. The first governing board consisted of J. W. Cheek as magistrate of police (later changed to mayor) and commissioners Robert F. Morris, A. M. Rigsbee, W. K. Styron, W. F. Clark, J. A. McMannen, and William Mangum.

Tiny Hillsborough was the seat of Orange County government when Durham had its birth. The increase of industry and the growth in population created a demand for functions of government that the local office could not fulfill; after all, Hillsborough was 15 miles away: property deeds had to be recorded there, and except for minor cases which local magistrates could handle, it was the nearest point for trials.

Something had to be done, and the leaders in Durham decided that a new county was the solution. Caleb Green, a member of the state legislature, favored the new county plan and introduced in 1881 a bill supported by the leading members of the community. Orange County, however, was bitterly opposed to the idea, for it meant the loss of its largest and most prosperous town. Other counties in the territory proposed for the new county also offered strong opposition.

Green's bill was defeated by the Senate, but its supporters did not give up the fight. As a result, the Senate reversed its action, and on February 28, 1881, the bill creating the new Durham County became law. On May 1, 1881, the people living within the proposed boundaries approved in a special election the formation of the county, and five men were chosen to serve as the first Durham County Board of Commissioners: A. K. Umstead, Washington Duke, G. A. Barbee, John T. Nichols, and S. W. Holman.

Back in the early years of its life, Durham was an unpretentious town. Dirt streets that were quagmires of mud after heavy rains extended in disorderly directions. High stepping-stones provided dry passage across the streets for pedestrians. All buildings were of wood in the beginning, but as the town grew, brick edifices began to rise in the business district. Disastrous fires played their part in removing wooden buildings, and no new wooden structures were built downtown after about 1900 in order to reduce risk of fire. Privies dotted the town. The water supply came from wells and ponds until 1887, when a city water system began operation under a private firm.

Soon after the turn of the century, on January 7, 1901, the leaders of the growing community decided that something had to be done to improve existing

Gray's 1881 map of Durham. By 1880 the population had grown to 2,041; only a decade earlier, it had been 256.

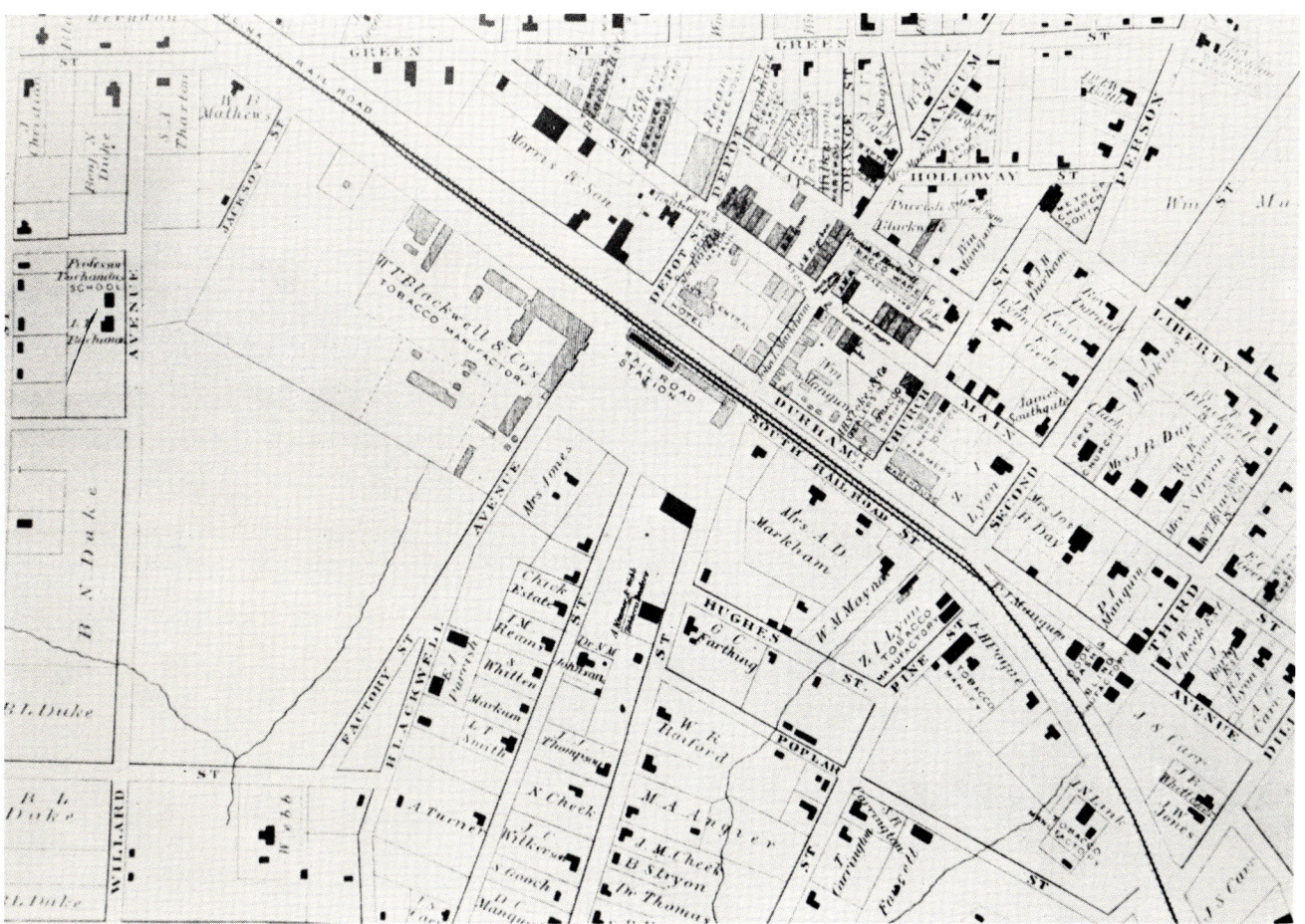

Map courtesy of Rare Book Room, Perkins Library, Duke University

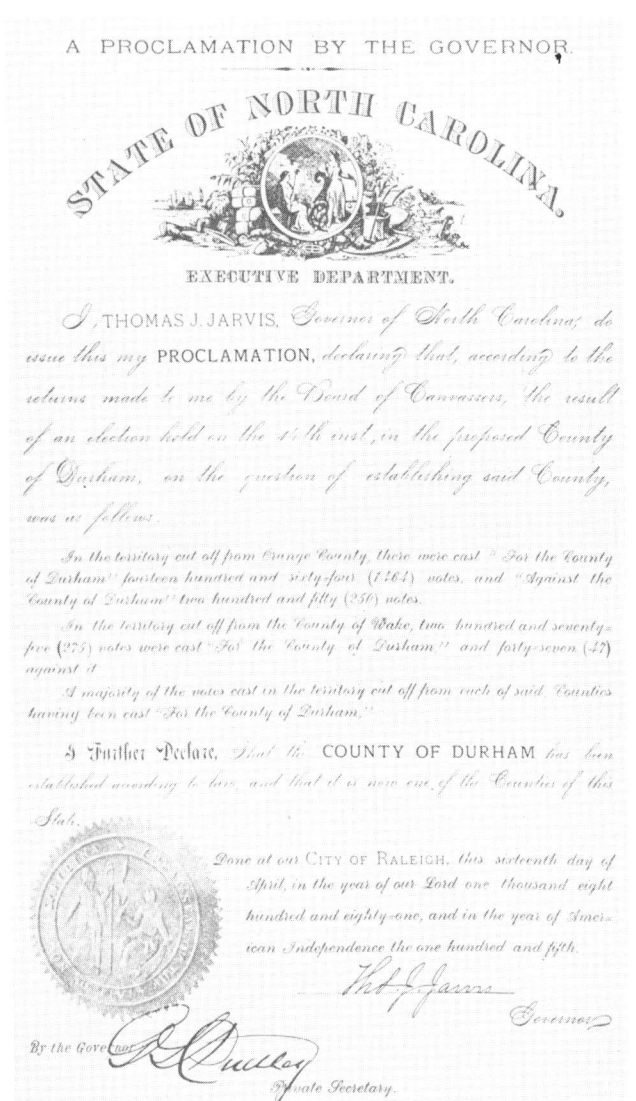

conditions. On that day an election was held to decide whether bonds should be issued to provide sidewalks, to improve streets, and to provide needed sewer facilities. The bonds were carried by the slim margin of 20 votes.

For five years after the founding of the sleepy little hamlet, it had no industries; life was quiet and easy. But, in 1858, things began to change. Robert F. Morris came from Granville County, firm in the belief that Durham had a bright future, and began the manufacture of smoking tobacco in a small wooden building on the site of the present mammoth plant of the American Tobacco Company. The trade name was "Best Flavored Spanish Smoking Tobacco." Business was good, but in 1862 Morris sold the company to John R. Green, who had moved to Durham from Person County. Green believed that the then-popular habit of chewing tobacco would give way, in time, to smoking, so he stored only the highest quality leaf for his smoking tobacco product. He began the manufacture of "Bull Durham" smoking tobacco, a brand destined to become the most popular and widely used product of its kind in the world.

As proclaimed in writing by Governor Thomas Jarvis in 1881, the County of Durham was formed from Wake and Orange Counties. In 1860, the town consisted of a railway station at the foot of what is now Corcoran Street, a post office, three stores, a carpenter shop, two bars, a tobacco factory, and a few houses.

In 1911, a part of Cedar Fork Township of Wake County was added to Durham County as Carr Township. No other additions or modifications have been made.

Photograph courtesy of Duke University Manuscript Department

Near Blackwell's Tobacco Factory at Jackson and Carr Streets looking west. Stacks of wood in the foreground along Carr Street were probably used for heating. Picket fences surround all of the properties. We can appreciate modern plumbing and water treatment facilities when we realize that the small buildings on the properties are outhouses. The first L-shaped house, left center, belonged to Captain Jack C. Michie, after whom Lake Michie was named. Dr. J. M. Manning, a Durham physician and one-time mayor of Durham, also lived in the area.

Photograph courtesy of Wyatt T. Dixon

John R. Green was the first to use a bull as his tobacco's trademark, and named his product "Bull Durham Smoking Tobacco." Such noted persons as Alfred, Lord Tennyson, and Prime Ministers William Gladstone and Benjamin Disraeli in England, would smoke the Bull Durham brand.

Photograph courtesy of State Division of Archives and History

"Durham Renowned the World Around"— symbolizing progress, health, wealth, and success in Durham. The sign, topped with an illuminated globe, was given to the city by the Durham Traction Company (the electric utility company) in an informal ceremony held on the night of December 15, 1913. Shortly afterward, the sign was blown down in a wind storm and never replaced. The building on which the sign was placed was located at the northeast corner of Main and Church Streets. In the left background is the steeple of Trinity Methodist Church.

Photograph courtesy of Wyatt T. Dixon

Robert F. Morris moved to Durham in 1858 and with his son operated Durham's first tobacco factory. Morris was prominent in Durham's political life, and he served as a member of the town's first board of town commissioners (1869) as well as a term as mayor.

Photograph courtesy of Wyatt T. Dixon

William T. Blackwell has been remembered for his influence on the industrialization and growth of the city. Blackwell's was the first large tobacco company in North Carolina, and his "Genuine Bull Durham" tobacco became known throughout the United States and Europe.

Portrait courtesy of Blackwell Brogden

W. Duke, Sons, and Company in 1883. Washington Duke's first home in Durham is at the left in this photograph taken facing north across the tracks of the North Carolina Railroad.

Photograph courtesy of Duke University Manuscript Department

As The War Between the States was nearing an end, business was good until seeming calamity struck. Soldiers of the North and South, in Durham during the Bennett Place meeting of Generals Johnston and Sherman, ransacked Green's factory and stole his tobacco. Green felt he was ruined. How wrong he was!

During the meeting of the two generals, the area near the tobacco plant was declared neutral ground, and soldiers of both sides mingled for friendly games and conversation. With the close of hostilities, they scattered to their homes in many sections of the nation, and soon orders began to pour in for more of "that good Durham tobacco."

William T. Blackwell and John R. Day became partners with Green in 1868, and with Green's death from tuberculosis a year later, Blackwell assumed the position of manager of the firm. In 1871, Julian S. Carr entered the business and provided the spark needed to build the Bull Durham plant into the world's largest smoking tobacco industry.

In 1865, Washington Duke, back from the war, had returned to his farm. A limited amount of tobacco had been overlooked by marauding soldiers, and in a small log cabin began the tobacco industry which was destined to become one of the largest. Duke's brand was "Pro Bono Publico," "for the public good." Two of Duke's sons, Benjamin N. and James B., joined their father in the business; Brodie L. Duke, the oldest of the three sons, was

manufacturing tobacco on his own.

Numerous tobacco factories sprang up, but with the formation of the American Tobacco Company by James B. Duke, they were either absorbed or were forced to close because they could not meet the competition. The American Tobacco Company eventually became so large that anti-trust and anti-monopoly suits were brought against it by the federal government. The company and its closely related subsidiaries were divided into the American Tobacco Company, Liggett and Myers Tobacco Company, P. Lorillard Company, and R. J. Reynolds Tobacco Company.

While the tobacco industry has dominated the industrial picture throughout the years, numerous other types of manufacturing have contributed to Durham's growing economy. Around the turn of the century, there were a snuff factory, a woolen mill, and plants for the manufacture of cigars, textiles, pants, boots, hosiery, shuttles for textile plants, and soap.

Durham is widely known as a major center of education, but such was not always the case. Efforts to provide the town with its first public graded school met opposition, but with the strong support of many of the leading citizens and the backing of parents who wanted to provide their children with better educational opportunities, the school opened its doors in Wright's Factory in 1882.

An important chapter in the cause of higher education began with the decision of the Methodist denomination to move little Trinity College from Randolph County and Durham's successful efforts to bring it here. In 1892, the college which has become Duke University opened its doors in Durham.

A new era in black education began when a Baptist minister, Dr. James E. Shepard, established the National Religious Training School. Today it is North Carolina Central University.

Today Durham is highly regarded as a major medical center, with many thousands of people coming to seek treatment in its numerous hospitals. The multi-million dollar Durham County General Hospital opened in 1977, and the mammoth Duke Hospital continues to expand, with a large addition begun in 1977. Other community medical facilities include McPherson Hospital, North Carolina Cerebral Palsy Hospital, and the Veterans Administration Hospital.

A doctor played a major role in providing the town with its first hospital. In 1872, Dr. Albert G. Carr began his practice of medicine here. Deeply concerned over local health conditions, he lost little time in beginning a crusade to correct them, but the fight for a hospital was not easily won. Dr. Carr was physician for George W. Watts, who had come to Durham to join the W. Duke and Sons tobacco company. In time Dr. Carr was successful in his efforts to arouse Watts' interest in his hospital project.

Watts was a man of action. Property at the northeast corner of Main Street and Buchanan Road was purchased, and a hospital was built at a total cost of $30,000. Watts gave an additional $20,000 as an endowment. At first the hospital was not a success; people regarded it as a place to come to die. In time, however, this feeling was dispelled, and patronage increased. Durham continued to grow, and the little hospital finally was unable to meet adequately the needs for its services.

Watts realized that a new hospital was needed. He purchased property in the western section of town, and on December 3, 1909, the new Watts Hospital opened its doors. As public demand for service grew, additions were made to the facility through the interest of Watts and his heirs.

Watts Hospital was used by white people only, and there was no place for blacks to go for treatment of their ailments. Here, again, a physician was instrumental in obtaining a hospital. Dr. Aaron Moore started a determined campaign to provide a facility for members of his race. He soon had the support of both white and black leaders, and success crowned his efforts when ground was broken in 1901 for a two-story building on Proctor Street, named Lincoln Hospital. In 1924 a new brick hospital was built on Fayetteville Street.

This brief introduction to the early origins of the community will help the reader appreciate the rich historical traditions surrounding Durham's inception and growth. The words and photographs that follow will present a treasured pictorial history of rare and contemporary photographs of a city of which its citizens are justly proud.

Duke Chapel as photographed in 1939. Novelist and scientist Aldous Huxley described the chapel as "the most successful essay in neo-Gothic that I know." The chapel tower, which overlooks not only the Duke University campus, but also most of Durham, stands 210 feet. In the 39 years since this photograph was taken, the trees have grown to great heights and the shrubs have matured.

Photograph courtesy of Wootten-Moulton Studio

George W. Watts donated the first hospital to Durham.

Photograph courtesy of State Division of Archives and History

The original Watts Hospital stood on a four-acre tract of land on the northeast corner of Main and Buchanan. Dedicated on February 21, 1895, it served the community over 14 years. Watts was the sixth general hospital in North Carolina, and the first in the state to receive an "A" rating from the American Medical Association, and its school of nursing is the second oldest in North Carolina. A new Watts Hospital on a 25-acre tract was dedicated on December 2, 1909, at a cost of $535,000, and served the city and county until the 1976 completion of the modern county hospital on North Roxboro Street.

Photograph courtesy of Wyatt T. Dixon

The central portion of the old Watts Hospital is now a private residence at 302 Watts Street, where it was moved from Main and Buchanan.

Photograph by Frank A. Kostyu

Lincoln Hospital on Fayetteville Street, now used on an outpatient basis, photographed in early 1978.

Photograph by Joel A. Kostyu

Plan of the City of Durham, North Carolina, at the turn of the century.

Map courtesy of Duke University Manuscript Department

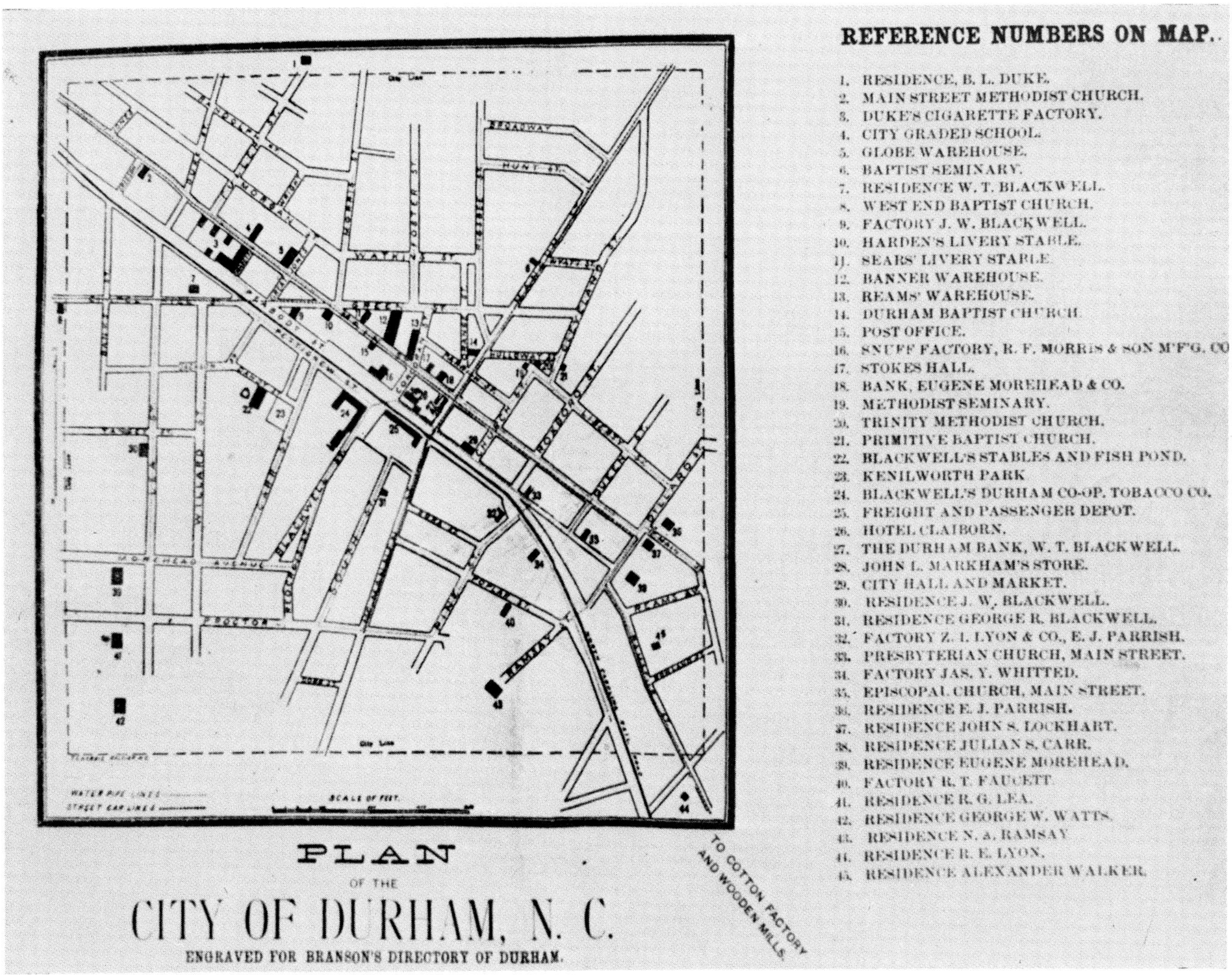

PLAN OF THE CITY OF DURHAM, N. C.
ENGRAVED FOR BRANSON'S DIRECTORY OF DURHAM.

REFERENCE NUMBERS ON MAP.

1. RESIDENCE, B. L. DUKE.
2. MAIN STREET METHODIST CHURCH.
3. DUKE'S CIGARETTE FACTORY.
4. CITY GRADED SCHOOL.
5. GLOBE WAREHOUSE.
6. BAPTIST SEMINARY.
7. RESIDENCE W. T. BLACKWELL.
8. WEST END BAPTIST CHURCH.
9. FACTORY J. W. BLACKWELL.
10. HARDEN'S LIVERY STABLE.
11. SEARS' LIVERY STABLE.
12. BANNER WAREHOUSE.
13. REAMS' WAREHOUSE.
14. DURHAM BAPTIST CHURCH.
15. POST OFFICE.
16. SNUFF FACTORY, R. F. MORRIS & SON M'F'G. CO.
17. STOKES HALL.
18. BANK, EUGENE MOREHEAD & CO.
19. METHODIST SEMINARY.
20. TRINITY METHODIST CHURCH.
21. PRIMITIVE BAPTIST CHURCH.
22. BLACKWELL'S STABLES AND FISH POND.
23. KENILWORTH PARK.
24. BLACKWELL'S DURHAM CO-OP. TOBACCO CO.
25. FREIGHT AND PASSENGER DEPOT.
26. HOTEL CLAIBORN.
27. THE DURHAM BANK, W. T. BLACKWELL.
28. JOHN L. MARKHAM'S STORE.
29. CITY HALL AND MARKET.
30. RESIDENCE J. W. BLACKWELL.
31. RESIDENCE GEORGE R. BLACKWELL.
32. FACTORY Z. I. LYON & CO., E. J. PARRISH.
33. PRESBYTERIAN CHURCH, MAIN STREET.
34. FACTORY JAS. Y. WHITTED.
35. EPISCOPAL CHURCH, MAIN STREET.
36. RESIDENCE E. J. PARRISH.
37. RESIDENCE JOHN S. LOCKHART.
38. RESIDENCE JULIAN S. CARR.
39. RESIDENCE EUGENE MOREHEAD.
40. FACTORY R. T. FAUCETT.
41. RESIDENCE R. G. LEA.
42. RESIDENCE GEORGE W. WATTS.
43. RESIDENCE N. A. RAMSAY.
44. RESIDENCE R. E. LYON.
45. RESIDENCE ALEXANDER WALKER.

BEGINNINGS

Durham is by some standards a young city. Yet, through rich oral traditions, archeological finds, extensive manuscript collections, and descriptive survey accounts, we can glimpse the early history of the land that later became known as Durham County.

The Eno, Flat, and Little Rivers, passing north of Durham, were essential to the development of the area. The water provided transportation and an adequate food source; it was used for various domestic purposes by the Indians that originally occupied the area. Five historic tribes or subgroups brought their own culture and language. The Tuscarora, a nomadic tribe, hunted in the region. The Eno, Shocco, Adshusheer, and Occaneechi, all of the Sioux nation, settled in villages and farmed.

The earliest recorded mention of the Eno Indians was by Francis Yardley in 1654. In 1670, John Lederer used the Great Indian Trading Path to make contact with the Occaneechi, Eno, and Shocco tribes, establishing a lucrative Piedmont trade route for furs. Lederer, visiting on what is now the Stagville tract, commented on the energetic, industrious nature of the Occaneechi: "...in their sports they exercise with so much labor and violence and in so great number, that I have seen the ground wet with the sweat that dropped off their bodies."

However, the encroachment of white traders threatened the commerce and lands used by the Occaneechi, and in 1673 it was reported that they killed an explorer named James Needham. Additional problems with the Occaneechi precipitated their massacre at the hands of Nathanial Bacon and others in 1673. The Occaneechi moved their settlement, Acconeechy, from the Dan and Roanoke Rivers (now under Kerr Lake) to near present-day Hillsborough. "Acconeechy" was the spelling used on Edward Moseley's 1733 Map of the Province of North Carolina.

Intertwined in this early history is the Great Indian Trading Path. From Petersburg, Virginia, to the Catawba and Waxhaw Indians in Carolina, it gave access to the uncharted Piedmont from about 1670 to fur traders, hunters, and explorers. Present day Interstate Highway 85 approximates the route of the Path in many places.

In 1701, John Lawson, Surveyor General of North Carolina, with Eno-Will, his guide and the leader of the Eno Indians, explored the Eno River region. He was greatly impressed with the hospitality, the beautiful landscape, and the potential for grist mills. Lawson made a particular point in his diary to remark about the unselfish, helpful nature of Eno-Will. Lawson, in 1711, died at the hands of the Tuscarora Indians, an occurrence which eventually led to the Tuscarora War and drove many Indians out of North Carolina.

Very little has been discovered about the Occaneechi after 1701. Their preoccupation with intertribal conflicts rather than the encroachments of the white man was undoubtedly a crucial factor in their leaving the region. Cultural finds of arrowheads of quartz and siliconized slate and bone tools in addition to metal trade knives and axes indicated a mixed acceptance of some of the new materials brought in by the whites. It is suspected that the Occaneechi joined the Saponi and the Tutelo in a move to the mouth of the Roanoke River. Records indicate that in 1722 they lived at Fort Christianna in Virginia. Again seeking protection, they joined the Iroquois in about 1740. In 1753 they were adopted by the Cayuga and became a member of the Six Nations. Waskiteng, the last known full-blooded Tutelo, died in 1871. No record of the last Occaneechian exists.

What is today Durham County was in the mainstream of North Carolina history from about 1750. William Johnston, a colonial merchant of Hillsborough and a kinsman of Royal Governor Gabriel Johnston, was a delegate to the Provincial Congress in 1775, which empowered him to forge iron for ammunition during the Revolution. He also operated a store on his Snow Hill plantation on Little River in what today is northern Durham County. Johnston was treasurer of the Transylvania Land Company, which sent Daniel Boone into the wilderness of Tennessee and Kentucky to explore. He is buried on Snow Hill plantation beneath a white marble ledger.

On May 9, 1771, Governor William Tryon and his elegantly uniformed and equipped army camped on New Hope Creek in the march to confront the Regulators at the famed Battle of Alamance. Tryon's army cut a road through the wilderness which he named the Ramsgate Road, but which Durhamites know today as Cornwallis Road.

The reverence of North Carolina for the cardinal, the state bird, was shared by the Occaneechi Indians. According to legend, Ulalee, a beautiful Occaneechi maiden living at Acconeechy on the Eno, delighted in spending hours with birds. One day near the river, a jealous lover stabbed her through the heart. Her blood discolored the water. The birds, grieving their dead friend, made loud harsh noises. The male of one species with a brown back and gray breast jumped into the red water; the mate used her bill to sprinkle drops on her breast and wings. Thus, according to legend, the male red bird is all red and the female only partly red. And, if you listen closely, you can hear them singing, "Ulalee-e-e."

Sketch from Eno River Calendar, 1976, from an engraving by Theodore DeBry

HERITAGE PRESERVED

"Somewhere in the midst of our industrial success, we almost lost a rich, fascinating chapter in the history of this state, and indeed, the nation," states a booklet on the Duke Homestead. A community such as Durham is ever-changing, and progress often necessitates the demolition of structures that have seemingly served their usefulness. But there has been a spirited change in thinking as Durham, like many other cities, is considering its heritage and taking positive strides to preserve some of its past. Organizations such as the Historic Preservation Society of Durham, the Downtown Revitalization Committee, the Association for the Preservation of the Eno River Valley, Friends of West Point, and the Trinity Park Association, along with numerous individuals, have rekindled community concern for Durham's heritage.

Five sites of historical interest are featured here: West Point on the Eno River, Hardscrabble Plantation, Stagville Plantation, Fairntosh Plantation, and the Duke Homestead. The latter four are on the National Register of Historic Places. They speak of the past while they remind us that the past is tied to the present and future, when those yet unborn will appreciate the heritage passed on to them. British historian Lord McCauley once wrote: "A people that takes no pride in the accomplishments of their remote ancestors will probably produce nothing worthy of recollection by their remote descendants."

Photograph courtesy of Wyatt T. Dixon

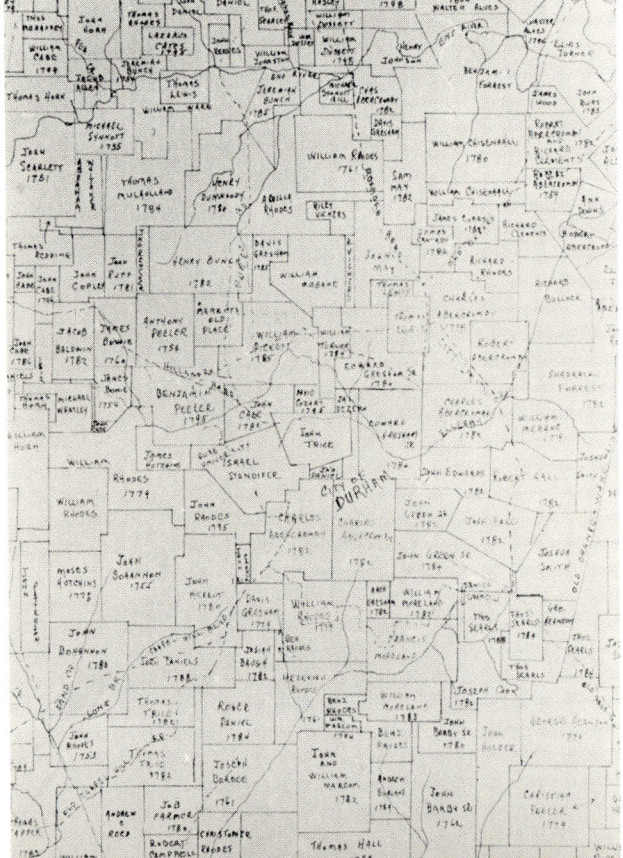

From a stencil used to label flour barrels, found in the rubble when the West Point mill was restored. Between 1873 and 1888, the time of the stamp, the mill belonged to William Lipscomb, one of ten owners whose names have been attached to the mill.

Stencil courtesy of Margaret Nygard

This land grant map facsimile, covering a period from 1743-1810, shows the area that is now Durham and the Eno River (top of map). Making the map was the late Allan B. Markham's hobby; he included various landmarks to aid identification.

*Map copyright© 1973 by Allan B. Markham,
Courtesy of Mrs. Allan B. Markham*

Eno River & West Point Mill

There have been a good many mills along the Eno River. "I remember Christians' Mill," wrote Mrs. Everett Roberts in 1972. "It was known as McCown's Mill, run by John Cabe McCown. There wasn't even a bridge there. Just above the bridge there was a ford. It was a mighty pretty ford when there wasn't a freshet on. Just across from the mill there was a liquor tavern, John Carrington's. I remember hearing them fighting in there."

One of the early millers on the Eno was Michael Synnott, a bachelor who, legend has it, kept half a pot of gold and silver in the mill. The river rose one day and carried him in and tumbled the mill into a deep hole. Through the years, people have been diving to get the pot of gold. Those who have made the attempt say they have never found the river bottom. Synnott was drowned and the whereabouts of the gold was never discovered.

The West Point mill operated from 1778 to 1942. The mill had several notable owners, including George Carrington, a Revolutionary soldier; Colonel Herbert Sims, a member of the General Assembly, militia officer, justice of the peace and rich landowner; John Cabe McCown; and Pressley J. Mangum, an early Durham postmaster, who moved to the Eno and West Point in 1888. His wife had a lovely garden. His son, Hugh, was a remarkable photographer whose darkroom was a barn and who left an extraordinary legacy of glass negatives depicting the people of his time as well as a stretch of the Eno River.

West Point mill, shown about 1895, collapsed in 1973 and is nearly restored as part of a 40-acre Eno River Park, dedicated in July, 1976.

West Point, probably photographed during the flood of 1908. The paintings on the building advertised the circus. Several structural changes had been made from the earlier photo.

Photograph courtesy of Margaret Nygard

Hardscrabble Plantation

Hardscrabble Plantation, covering 600 acres, is the oldest plantation house in Durham County, located five miles northwest of Durham on St. Mary's Road. The oldest section of the house was built by William and Elizabeth Clenny around 1775. James Cain and his son John, who bought the plantation four years later, added a second dwelling about 1792. It was then essentially two houses joined by a breezeway.

Later, the plantation passed to William Cain, another son of James Cain. William was a generous benefactor to the University of North Carolina and a member of the General Assembly. His daughter, Charity Alston Cain, was married to Willie Person Mangum, one of Durham County's most famous sons. After serving in congress as a Whig (1823), Mangum became a superior court judge (1827). Elected to the United States Senate in 1830, he served as president pro tempore from 1842-45. By virtue of his office, he was next in line to the presidency after Vice President John Tyler took office following the death of President William H. Harrison. He left the Senate in 1853, retiring to his Walnut Hall plantation in what is now Durham County. He died a heart-broken man on September 7, 1861, five weeks after the death of his only son in the Civil War.

After William Cain's death in 1834, his son William, II, who was married to the sister of Chief Justice Thomas Ruffin, lived in the house until his death in 1857. At that time, his son Dr. James F. Cain took possession, giving the name Hardscrabble to the plantation, which was in contrast to the "care free" designation of Sans Souci, built by William Cain, II, in Hillsborough in 1913.

Hardscrabble has been restored by Dr. and Mrs. Roscoe Strickland, Jr.

Photograph by Joel A. Kostyu

Fairntosh Plantation

Fairntosh was begun in 1810 by Duncan Cameron, planter, banker, judge of the Superior Court, and leader of the Whig Party. He named his estate after the Scottish village from which his father came to America. The magnificent plantation house was built in a Georgian-Federal transitional style, and the handsome porch with Greek Revival decoration was added in 1827. This estate became the largest plantation in North Carolina and worked over 500 slaves in the ante-bellum period. Judge Cameron's son, Paul, inherited the estate in 1853, and before his

Stagville Plantation

death in 1891, was the richest man in the state. In 1875 Paul Cameron reopened the University of North Carolina, which had closed in 1871 due to the aftermath of the Civil War, and paid the faculty out of his own pocket. He was a noted agriculturist and a railroad official. His son, Bennehan Cameron, was the last Cameron by name to own Fairntosh. Bennehan Cameron's daughter, Sally Labouisse, sold the estate in 1974 to Mr. and Mrs. William A. McFarland, who operate the 3,600-acre plantation.

Photograph courtesy of State Division of Archives and History

Stagville, seven miles north of Durham on the Old Oxford Road, was the home of Richard Bennehan (1747-1825), a well-to-do planter, merchant, early trustee of the University of North Carolina, and commissioner to lay out the city of Raleigh. Bennehan entertained many influential men at his home, including: General William R. Davie, ambassador to France and founder of the University at Chapel Hill; William Hooper, signer of the Declaration of Independence; James Iredell, U. S. Supreme Court Justice; and Archibald DeBow Murphey, pioneer in education in the state.

The present plantation house was begun in 1787 and enlarged in the 1790's. Bennehan's only daughter, Rebecca, married Duncan Cameron in 1803, and in 1810 they settled at neighboring Fairntosh. After Richard Bennehan's death the plantation passed to his only son, Thomas, and at his death in 1847 it went to Paul Cameron of Fairntosh, and was a major division of what became the largest plantation in North Carolina. Stagville numbered several thousand acres in 1847.

In 1860 there were over 500 slaves listed by name in the Cameron family registers, and the black history of the Stagville-Fairntosh tracts is nationally significant. The eminent historian Herbert Gutman stated that the material history of the American black at Stagville was "irreplaceable." Alex Haley, author of *Roots*, serves on the Stagville Preservation Center Advisory Committee, as do a number of nationally prominent preservationists.

In 1950 the Stagville plantation of about 3,000 acres was sold out of the Cameron family, and in 1954 it was purchased by the Liggett and Myers Tobacco Company (now the Liggett Group, Inc.), and in 1976 they deeded 71 acres to the State of North Carolina to establish the Stagville Preservation Center, the nation's first state-owned center for the teaching of historic preservation and its related technology. The Bennehan House serves as the center's headquarters, and other agricultural buildings are used as laboratory buildings in the center's program.

Photograph by Joel A. Kostyu

Washington Duke stands at the door of the log barn that was the first Duke tobacco factory. Thirty feet long by 20 feet wide, it burned and has been reconstructed.

Photograph courtesy of State Division of Archives and History

The rebuilt Duke family tobacco factory, viewed here through tobacco plants.

Photograph by Frank A. Kostyu

Duke Homestead

The Dukes went back to visit the homestead in the early 1900's.

Photograph courtesy of Duke University Manuscript Department

The Duke Homestead was seriously run-down until the family rallied to save it. Through the generosity of Mrs. Mary Duke Biddle, granddaughter of Washington Duke, and other family members and friends, Duke University purchased the farm in 1931. It was restored as nearly as possible to its earlier condition and refurnished with period furniture, some of which were in the original dwelling.

The house, built in 1852, contained four rooms—two downstairs and two upstairs, plus a kitchen that was actually a separate log cabin behind the house. When the family grew, the kitchen was replaced with an addition of another kitchen and an "old folks room" attached to the rear of the structure.

Duke Homestead reflects the Duke family just after the Civil War. The site includes the main house, the reconstructed first factory, the original third factory, and two outstanding outbuildings. On Sunday, April 28, 1968, a ceremony was held to designate the property as a National Historic Landmark. The Homestead, owned by Duke University for 43 years, was given to the state of North Carolina in 1974.

Photograph by Frank A. Kostyu

The pack-house was built in the early 1900's, after the Dukes had moved to Durham. The tobacco was brought from the curing barn to this building, where the leaves were stripped from the stalk, graded, and bundled. The bundles of leaves were then packed away and stored until there was enough to take to the market.

Photograph by Frank A. Kostyu

The second tobacco factory has been destroyed. However, the third, an unpainted frame structure, is visible from the Duke Homestead bedroom.

Photograph by Frank A. Kostyu

THE CIVIL WAR

The Civil War had a dramatic effect on the development of Durham. Durham, known earlier by the names Durhamville, Durham's Station, Durham's and finally Durham, was a small village of less than 100 people that grew up around a depot of the North Carolina Railroad. With the military surrender of Confederate General Joseph E. Johnston to Union General William T. Sherman at Bennett Place west of Durham on April 26, 1865, 17 days after Robert E. Lee's surrender at Appomattox, the convulsion that rocked the country was brought to a close in the Carolinas, Georgia, and Florida. The Union and Confederate soldiers who raided the leaf houses storing bright leaf tobacco advertised the unique tobacco to the rest of the country, and opportunities for industry were born.

Before the Civil War there was no real industry in agricultural Durham. The section of the railroad that supplied Durham had little bearing on the war effort. Heated debates had taken place for and against secession. Even those like Washington Duke and Senator Willie P. Mangum, who opposed secession, cast their lot with the Confederacy. Many came back from the war virtually penniless. However, Durham prided itself in having "no aristocracy but the aristocracy of labor" and later prospered on the foundations of its new tobacco industry.

General William Tecumseh Sherman (1820-1891). When Grant became President of the United States in 1869, Sherman replaced him as supreme commander of the U. S. Army, with the rank of full general. In a speech in 1880, he succinctly summed up his experiences. He said: "War...is...hell."

Photograph courtesy of State Division of Archives and History

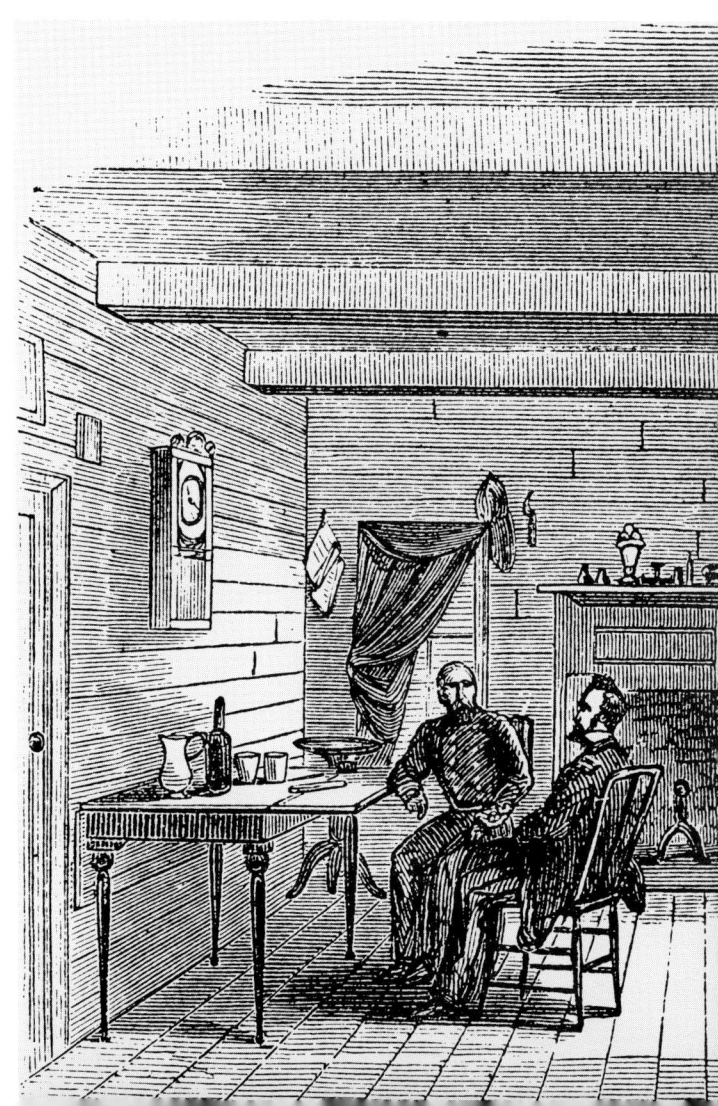

A drawing of the meeting of Johnston, left, and Sherman in the Bennett home. From Greensboro, Johnston had sent a request for negotiations to Sherman, who had entered Raleigh on April 13, 1865, and the two planned to meet on April 17 at a point midway between the picket lines of the opposing armies.

On the morning of April 17, Sherman took a train from Raleigh, arriving in Durham's Station at 10 a.m. Accompanied by a squadron of cavalry and following a horseman bearing a white flag, Sherman rode out of Durham upon the Hillsborough Road until he encountered General Johnston. Johnston told Sherman of a farmhouse he had passed where they might hold discussions, and the two generals retired to this house. The house was the Bennett Place.

General Joseph Eggleston Johnston (1807-1891). In July 1864, as he was preparing to fight William Sherman's Union Army, Jefferson Davis relieved him of his command. He was recalled in 1865 in a futile effort to stop Sherman's march through North Carolina, but surrendered to Sherman on April 26. After the war, Johnston served one term as a U. S. Congressman.

Photograph courtesy of State Division of Archives and History

Johnston was ordered by Jefferson Davis, who opposed the more stringent terms of the plan of surrender, to disband the infantry and make an escape with the mounted troops as quickly as possible. Johnston, realizing the tragedy of a prolonged war, however, disobeyed orders and met Sherman again at the Bennett Place on April 26.

Johnston and Sherman, after their meeting at Bennett Place, were to become friends. When Sherman died in 1891, Johnston was an honorary pallbearer at the funeral. It rained on that day, and Johnston, though urged to keep his hat on, would not. He caught pneumonia and died a few weeks later.

Drawing courtesy of State Division of Archives and History

The Bennett Place has been named a State Historical Site and is listed on the National Register of Historic Places. A suitable marker designates the important site.

Photograph by Frank A. Kostyu

The Bennett Place years after Johnston and Sherman met there in April, 1865. The photo pre-dates by a few years the fire that was to burn the house in the fall of 1921. The house is on the left, while the building on the right was used as a kitchen.

Photograph courtesy of Mr. and Mrs. George C. Pyne, Jr.

The bottle from which the generals drank and toasted one another after completing negotiations. The table on which the bottle rests was also in the room in which the generals conferred. Both of these mementos are in the possession of Southgate Jones, Jr.

Photograph courtesy of State Division of Archives and History

The landmark monument at Bennett Place was erected in 1923 through the "generosity of Mrs. S. T. Morgan and the auspices of the Durham-Orange County Historical Society." The two columns represent the North and the South. The frieze across the top has carved into it "Unity."

Photograph by Frank A. Kostyu

Bennett Place in 1977. Through the efforts of R. O. Everett, chairman of the Durham-Orange Historical Society, the Bennett Place was rebuilt in 1961. Hubert Humphrey visited Bennett Place in 1965 to commemorate the one hundred year anniversary of the signing of the peace treaty.

Photograph by Frank A. Kostyu

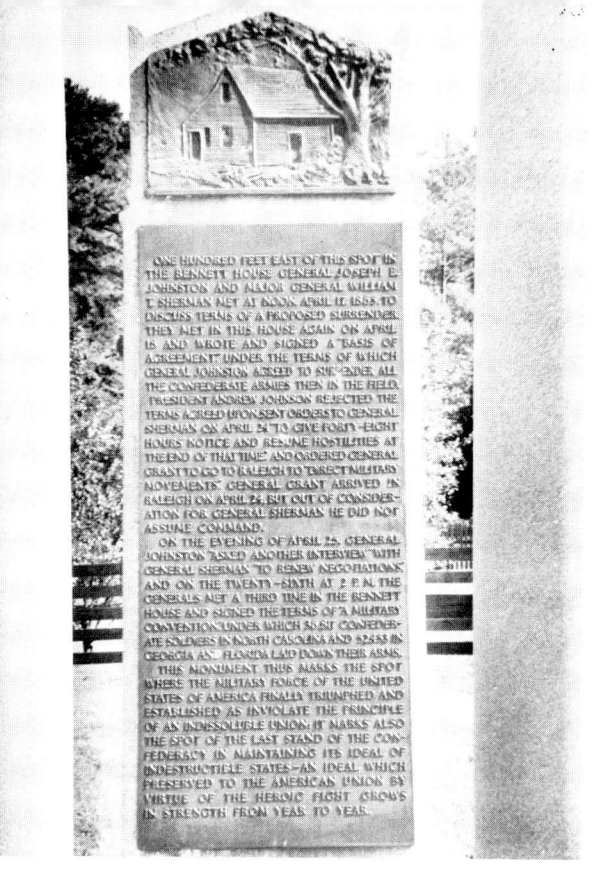

Confederate veterans pose in front of the Hotel Carrolina during a May 10 Confederate Memorial Day celebration, about the turn of the century.

Photograph courtesy of Wyatt T. Dixon

This early 1920's photograph shows a reunion of Confederate veterans at Bennett Place.

Photograph courtesy of Wyatt T. Dixon

The Confederate veterans' reunion around 1923 at Bennett Place attracted a large crowd of Durham residents to hear Julian S. Carr. The chimney was all that remained after the fire in 1921.

Photograph courtesy of Wyatt T. Dixon

The Alex Dickson home on the old Hillsborough Road was the headquarters of General Joseph E. Johnston during peace negotiations at the Bennett Place. The house was restored by Mrs. William Preston Few, wife of Duke University's first president.

Photograph courtesy of Wyatt T. Dixon

This small building on the farm of Alex Dickson on old Hillsborough Road was used by General Johnston in 1865 as his office during the conferences at Bennett Place.

Photograph courtesy of Wyatt T. Dixon

The house of William Mangum at the corner of Chapel Hill Street and Rigsbee Avenue was General William T. Sherman's headquarters during the surrender proceedings at Bennett Place. The post office now stands on the site.

Photograph courtesy of Wyatt T. Dixon

REMINISCENCES OF A DURHAM CHILDHOOD: THE TURN OF THE CENTURY

By Elsie Wallace Perkins

In bicentennial 1976, our collective thoughts turned backward to earlier times in our nation's history. My own thoughts returned to former days in our own community, this spot we call Durham. Perhaps you might be interested in knowing what Durham was like, roughly from the turn of the century until about 1918.

My recollections are not the result of scientific or historical research. Rather, they are the impressions and memories of a pig-tailed, spindly legged, happy little girl growing up in an average Southern town, a town recovering from the Civil War in a nation not yet embroiled in the first of the great wars that would touch everyone's life.

Durham started out as a pretty rough town. With saloons abounding, the community regarded brawls and knifings and general rowdiness as common occurrences. Ladies did not walk unaccompanied on the streets, for one never knew when a body would come hurtling through a saloon door. But by the turn of the century, thanks largely to the efforts of the Women's Christian Temperance Union, these establishments had vanished or had gone underground. Churches sprang up everywhere, and they, plus the banks and the schools, gave the town an aura of respectability.

As I remember it, Durham was rather charming. If all the people in Hope Valley, Duke Forest, Croasdaile, Willowhaven, and points between had been living in well-kept houses on East Main Street, on McMannen Street, on Rigsbee Avenue, on Mangum Street, on Broadway, on Morris Street, on Holloway Street, and on Dillard Street, some idea could be gained of the way we all lived happily and closely together. Those streets were filled with ladies and gentlemen and assorted children *walking* from place to place. After all, everyone went to church many, many times during the week, with two services on Sunday, prayer meeting on Wednesday, and choir practice on Thursday. We walked downtown for the evening mail; we walked uptown to shop.

The swishing long skirts of the ladies swept up the dust. The men always covered their heads with derbies, bowlers, fedoras, or, in the summer, straw hats. I personally have felt the world has never been the same since the men discarded that badge of chivalry, the hat. There was something decidedly graceful in the upswing of a man's arm as he swept off his chapeau, sometimes even to a little girl. How proud she felt, and she walked a little straighter and pointed her long chin just a little higher as she hurried to the meat market for a pound of steak for supper. The prince of all the hat-doffers was Dr. William Preston Few, president of Trinity College. He knew every coed and always swept off that soft felt hat with the most courtly gesture imaginable.

People walked and smiled and said, "Good morning," or, after twelve o'clock, "Good evening," even though one had not the foggiest notion of who

Elsie Wallace Perkins is a pseudonym for a long-time resident of Durham. She originally titled her manuscript "The Meanderings of An Old Lady," explaining: "You know, we never quarrel or challenge the rambling stories of the very old. We smile and murmur, 'How interesting!' and let their preposterous tales give them the satisfactions they crave." Readers will not agree with Ms. Perkins' view in this regard, for she has captured a spirit of Durham that is a delight to read and recall.

May 10, circa 1900, was observed as Confederate Memorial Day. A parade was the big event. This view is from in front of the Southern Conservatory of Music toward Main Street. Note the open carriages and the decorated horses.

Photograph courtesy of Wyatt T. Dixon

The old Trinity Church in a postcard dating around 1910. The church burned on Sunday morning, January 21, 1923.

Postcard courtesy of Stephen Massengill

the individual addressed might be. We were taught it was considerate to speak.

The unpaved streets were filled with all manner of horse- or mule-drawn conveyances, elegant carriages, and wagons. The people from the country rode in their wagons, conscious of the difference in their way of life from that of the city folk. Bringing fresh vegetables, cotton, or tobacco, they had a different look from that of the city dwellers. And always, in the very center of the street, the streetcars clanged their way from one end of the small town to the other.

Durham was indeed small. Going east and west, its boundaries were, in the east, the beginnings of the Edgemont community, marked by the Golden Belt factory; about where Watts Street begins was the western edge; the north extended to the bridge that goes above the railroad tracks on Mangum Street; the southern border could be placed at what was McMannen Street, now the extension of Mangum Street.

The peripheral areas were communities unto themselves rather than part of the town. The campus of Trinity College reposed in splendid isolation, surrounded by young trees and great vistas of space. West Durham was a village entirely separated from Durham. Its inhabitants and those of the Pearl Mill Village on what was later to be Trinity Avenue were referred to as "mill folks," and they supposedly basked under the patriarchal protection of W. A. Erwin and George Watts. Edgemont, as always, was the hosiery mill village under the sponsorship of the Carr family. Beyond Edgemont lay East Durham that thousands of people have loved and called home.

To the southeast was the great sprawling community of black people called Hayti. Most of the cooks, maids, gardeners, and handymen lived in that area.

Main Street in those years was a busy and cheerful place. Money was being made, impressive banks were being erected, business was booming. Shopping with my mother was a real pleasure. On those trips a person met old friends and picked up juicy bits of news; chatting with the sales ladies, all of them well known in the community, was fascinating. A choice between going to G. E. Rawles, approximately where the Roscoe Griffin Shoe Store was, to Kronheimers, where Rose's store is today, was offered. These large, well-stocked "dry goods" stores had bolts of cloth mounting to the rafters. These were the days when ladies' garments were made at home or by a local dressmaker. Cloth, trimmings, and patterns were staples. Besides the cloth needed, women bought soutasch braid, bombazine, jet beading, ostrich feathers, fancy buttons called entredeaux, sheer muslin, nainsook, sturdy long cloth, fancy laces, filmy and seductive veiling, whalebone, rats for a pompadour, high buttoned shoes, heavy black silk stockings, or, bliss

of all blisses, taffeta petticoats. Little wire baskets glided high above shoppers' heads on trolley-like wires, transferring articles to and from the clerks.

Sometimes the "show girls," in Durham for some play or musical comedy at the Academy of Music, could be seen. These girls, exotic creatures, had eyes heavy with mascara; the forbidden rouge and lipstick were heavily applied. Their clothing, drenched in perfume, was straight out of New York. Since no matinee occupied their time, they toured the local stores out of sheer boredom. I stared at them in utter fascination and thought how exciting the life of a showgirl must be.

Mr. Bernard's drug store dispensed the B.C. Headache Powder remedy. Mr. Bernard, an ascetic bachelor, happily presided over his medicinal paraphernalia. Young blades of Durham, suffering from the torments of hangovers, would rush into the store and wail, "Mr. Bernard, for God's sake fix me up something to take away this headache—quick!" Men in Durham swore by it, and soon it gained wide popularity. At this point, Mr. Council entered the picture. He had the money for the mass production of the remedy and for extensive advertising. Soon the famous B.C. Remedy found its way across the United States.

Opposite the present Wachovia Bank building stood the Post Office, an imposing mass of granite with broad, sweeping steps leading up to (wonder of wonders) revolving doors, the first seen anywhere in these parts. The most pleasant thing I recall about the Post Office was the free performances held on the steps to advertise visiting minstrel shows, so popular during that era. The idea was that after hearing the jazz band and rich male voices of the chorus, together with a joke or two, listeners would rush down to the Academy of Music and purchase tickets for the night's performance. Though not permitted to attend the evening show, nothing kept me from enjoying those free performances on the Post Office steps.

Every small town of the era had its hat stores; Durham had two—the Misses Albright's establishment and that of Mrs. Piper. Oh! What beautiful hats! Walking into those stores was like strolling through a flower garden. Nothing has ever surpassed them in beauty and grandeur. Each hat had its own pedestal and plenty of space for admirers to view it. The hat boxes were tremendous, with generous sheets of tissue paper tenderly cradling the exotic creations to be transported in them. And how I loved the veils! Women looked alluring as they were swathed in some flattering shade of sheer chiffon or were wearing a saucy black nose-tip veil.

My favorite store was the candy store that stood approximately next to what is now the Duke Power Company building. It was a real, honest-to-goodness candy store run by two Greek men. In the front were cases and cases of mouth-watering confections of

An early view of the Trinity College campus on land formerly known as Blackwell Park, owned by Julian S. Carr. Craven Memorial Building is at the right; the library is behind Craven; the Mary Duke Dormitory is on the left. The track was formerly used for horse races at the park.

Photograph courtesy of Duke University Manuscript Department

Unpaved streets abounded in early Durham. This street was "faculty row" for Trinity College.

Photograph courtesy of Duke University Archives

Many remember the styles of past years, but only a few will recall the type of hat Mamie Dowd Walker is wearing in this photograph. The snow owl is rare in North Carolina.

Photograph courtesy of Mr. and Mrs. George C. Pyne, Jr.

Muirhead Plaza, formerly Five Points, shown here looking west with Main Street on the right and Chapel Hill Street on the left, has always been a focus of traffic in Durham. Shown here is the Five Points Drug Company in the 1920's. In this location, Mr. Bernard and Mr. Council produced the BC Headache Remedy. Today a restaurant building occupies this spot.

Photograph courtesy of Duke University Manuscript Department

every kind. I often glimpsed, in the back, the great copper kettles used to boil the sweet syrup. Occasionally I could see a machine with great revolving arms, pulling taffy. My choice of the many delights was always the chocolate nougat, so deliciously melting on the tongue, the crunchy white almonds to be savored last. I could also purchase another favorite, a colorful sundae, new and extremely popular, and sit at a little metal table, watching the world go by as the sweet concoction trickled down my throat.

There were no vacant stores. Every other site was filled with shoe stores, men's clothing stores, jewelry, and imposing banks.

The railroad station at the foot of Church Street was a busy place, with travelers arriving and departing on passenger trains. Huge engines puffed out white clouds of steam. Vast and cavernous, the tiled floors of the station were wonderful for little girls and boys to slide on. Travelers brought great trunks that had to be carted to their various destinations. Lindsey Faucette was a familiar figure, with his horse-drawn dray, clattering over the cobblestones of Church Street to stores and homes all over Durham as he delivered the trunks of the drummers and the visitors.

A particularly fond memory of Main Street is that of the library, situated at Five Points, where the park of a thousand bricks now stands. It was just a house, a rather drab house, but to me it was a wondrous place. There I worked my way through the primers, the Bobbsey Twins, the Hardy series, sentimental love stories, and all the Westerns ever written. Some day we shall point with pride at our steel and glass library, but nothing can ever replace my nostalgia for that shabby house at Five Points.

One of the greatest contributors to the cultural life of Durham was the Southern Conservatory of music. Run by Mr. and Mrs. Gilmore Ward Bryant, this school for music students was housed in a rather large residence at the corner of Main and Duke Streets across the street from one of the Duke homes. The Bryants promoted good music in Durham; their students ranged from boarders from all over the state, intent on getting a degree in music, to fledgling youngsters of Durham encouraged in the art of piano playing by ambitious mothers. Never shall I forget the big practice hall or the cacophony of sounds filling it when all the little practice rooms were engaged by piano or voice students, all playing different tunes or trilling up and down the scales with varying degrees of fervor. I recall the excitement

Main Street looking east from Corcoran Street, from a picture postcard made around 1910. The first building on the right was the First National Bank, managed by Julian S. Carr. The electric streetcar had come to Durham in 1902.

Postcard courtesy of Duke University Manuscript Department

Looking from the corner of Main and Corcoran Streets are the old Post Office, demolished in 1934, and the Trust Building, with the Washington Duke Hotel in the background. The photograph dates to the late 1920's.

Photograph courtesy of Wyatt T. Dixon

of recitals when nervous boys and girls dressed in their starched best waited to prove (or disprove) their ability. One seldom hears of the Bryants today, but their contribution to the cultural life of Durham lives on through the inspired music teachers who carry on their dedication to good music.

Many of the beautiful houses of the period are almost forgotten—the Carr house, across from the East Main Street highrise apartment building; the Toms house, where the bus station is now located; the houses on Dillard Street; the Erwin and the E. K. Powe houses on West Main Street; the Watts and Morehead houses; the various Duke houses—all were classic examples of the architecture of the time.

It is true that the tobacco odor wafted through Durham, for the factory windows were wide open in the summer, and one could see the workers toiling over the yellow leaves of the plant and could hear the clanking of the machines. I can recall the chant of the black workers in the old factory on Main Street, not necessarily from joy but rather as a way to ease the monotony of the long hours of going through the same motions day in and day out. The supervisor, eager to increase his weekly quota, encouraged the workers in their chanting. I remember the perfect cadence, the often eerie and

Durham's first public library was located at Five Points at Chapel Hill and Main Streets. The lot for the building was donated by Lallah Ruth Carr, a member of the Canterbury Club, which was largely responsible for raising funds for the building. When it opened its doors on February 1, 1898, the wooden structure was the first free public library in North Carolina. Later the Piedmont Building occupied the site. A small park has taken its place. The old frame building was replaced in 1921 by the Carnegie Library on East Main Street. A new library is under construction.

Photograph courtesy of Wyatt T. Dixon

The second factory of W. Duke, Sons, and Company in Durham was erected in 1885.

Photograph courtesy of Duke University Manuscript Department

strangely moving rhythms of the tunes.

One sight peculiar to Durham was the great number of sacks delivered to the doors of many families each week. The Bull Durham factory had hit upon a method of selling tobacco in inexpensive little muslin bags with little yellow drawstrings at the top coupled with a packet of tissue paper squares. What the machines could not do was to attach a little cardboard disc stating that inside the bag could be found Bull Durham tobacco of highest quality. The bull trademark on the tag attested to that. Here many families could earn a few dollars each week attaching the tags to the bags, using the same looping one finds on price tags of garments in shops today. Tagging sacks was fun as we sat before an open fire on a cold winter afternoon while someone told ghost stories.

Men with maimed and broken bodies were a cruel reminder of a war that had ended just 35 years before. I saw those casualties, great, disfiguring scars across faces, men with arms and legs missing, the shuffling blind, the beggars asking for coins.

We often forget the great contribution the medical profession has made in correcting such birth deformities as hare-lips, crossed eyes, club feet, cleft palates. The sight of people so afflicted was not uncommon in those early days. Many of the mill people had a strange, whitish pallor resulting from the poor working conditions and the lack of medical attention.

Two sights I recall quite vividly occurred on Mangum Street. One was an old, old woman, fiercely independent and not caring a whit what the

The famed Bull Durham bag. A small round tag was attached to the string at the top.

Drawing courtesy of Liggett-Myers Company

43

world might think of her as she marched her cows up the street to a pasture about where Duke Park is today. To me she seemed like a gray ghost—her clothes were a shapeless shrouding of her stooped figure, her shoes heavy brogans, her hair thin and gray, screwed into a tight knot atop her head. She would look neither to the right nor to the left, only at those four or five loping cows she drove before her.

The second sight was a much more pleasant one. Captain Edward J. Parrish had but recently returned from several years in Japan as representative of the American Tobacco Company. He had built for himself a beautiful, white-columned house out on the Roxboro Road. Captain Parrish was a dashing figure of a man, with his white hair, his modish white goatee, and his immaculate white suits lending an air of elegance to this financially successful gentleman. Mrs. Parrish was just as elegant, with pretty flouncy dresses and the tiniest of lace parasols shading her features. Several times a week in the summer, the couple would ride by in their brougham, the top lowered and the driver correct in his livery, proudly guiding the handsome bays down the street at a leisurely pace.

My first introduction to sin occurred on Main Street. Durham had a famous prostitute, and I clearly recall her promenade down Main Street in the afternoon. I had been sent to the new Great Atlantic and Pacific Tea Company store to buy two pounds of brown sugar, obtained from a big burlap bag, and a pound of coffee beans. The store had a delightfully spicy scent, and I enjoyed being dispatched on such an errand. It was then that I first saw the notorious lady. I had been told she was an "evil" woman and that I was expected to scorn her. But how could one scorn such a gorgeous creature, quite tall, with a superb figure, dressed in the latest fashion! She strolled along with an assured, almost arrogant gait. Her eyes appeared to glitter with disdain as she looked at the dowdy women who shunned her as they passed. She could have blackmailed half the men in town, and this knowledge gave her an air of assurance that manifested itself in her erect and haughty carriage. I was agog with excitement!

I cannot write of old Durham and omit Lakewood Park. Situated roughly where Lakewood Shopping Center is now located, the park was the summer gathering-place for all of Durham. Families took along picnic suppers with great hampers of fried chicken, pimiento sandwiches, ham biscuits, homemade pickles, pies, and cakes. Most people rode on the summer street cars, a delightful experience. The seats, covered in rattan, ran straight across the car, and the summer breezes blew at will. The conductor walked along a narrow platform on the side of the car and collected the fares. The car rode straight out Chapel Hill Road, and it seemed such a long, long journey. Wonderful sounds could be heard as we approached the park. The merry-go-round attracted the small fry, and patient fathers held onto the little ones as they rode the gilded horses. For the emancipated teenagers there was a roller skating rink with its steady roar of wheels going round and round in monotonous circles. For the older boys and girls, the dating crowd, was the pavilion where they could dance to canned but current music. Little girls would crowd in, their eyes aglow and envious, dreaming of the time they too could get out on that floor with some Romeo and become belles of the ball. After all the activities were over and after stuffing themselves on the contents of the picnic baskets, pleasantly tired Durham residents would again board the streetcar and return home, feeling that a glamorous evening had ended too soon.

This was Durham, seen through the eyes of a little girl between the years of 1900 and 1918, a never-to-be-forgotten era recalled fondly and with nostalgia.

Edward J. Parrish was in the tobacco warehouse business in the later part of the nineteenth century. Later, he worked in the Far East as a representative for the American Tobacco Company.

Photograph courtesy of Wyatt T. Dixon

The Southern Conservatory of Music, at the southwest corner of Main and Duke Streets, was opened in 1898 and operated by Gilmore Ward Bryant. It was torn down in the 1930's, and a parking lot now occupies the site.

Photograph courtesy of Wyatt T. Dixon

INDUSTRY & COMMERCE

Durham is located in the greatest tobacco-growing area of the world. The industrial development began with the discovery in 1858 that the soil would produce a fine, bright tobacco. Robert F. Morris and his son grew a few tobacco plants, shredded their leaves, and peddled them in eastern North Carolina. Early tobacco factories were operated by John R. Green, who bought out Morris in 1862, and William T. Blackwell, whose product was named "Bull Durham."

W. Duke, Sons, and Company started making cigarettes in 1881. In 1884 it became the first cigarette manufacturer to mechanize, utilizing the Bonsack machine. In the price war that followed, many small tobacco concerns were absorbed, and W. Duke, Sons, and Company grew into the giant American Tobacco Company.

The growth of the tobacco industry spawned other industries. Cotton mills that made bags for the tobacco branched out into the production of chambrays, ginghams, sheets, pillowcases, and hosiery. Julian S. Carr, the Duke family, W. A. Erwin, J. H. Erwin, and George W. Watts contributed significantly to the development of Durham's cotton industries. In 1888 Eugene Morehead and Samuel T. Morgan organized the Durham Fertilizer Company. In 1893 came the Durham Soap Works; the Wortham Wooden Mills manufactured sashes, doors, blinds, mantels, and general house furnishings.

The printing plant of H. E. Seeman provided labels and bands for cigarette packages; the Seeman Carriage Company produced hand-made vehicles; R. T. Howerton manufactured caskets and coffins. Banks, merchants, utilities, transportation and mercantile establishments moved into the community.

This industrial expansion continued to develop with the establishment of the famed Research Triangle Park, a 5,400-acre campus for research-oriented industries which lies principally in Durham County.

Leaf houses like this were common throughout Durham in the 1880's and 1890's. This one belonged to Brodie L. Duke. He and his son Brodie Lawrence were active in the tobacco business.

Photograph courtesy of Duke University Manuscript Department

The Globe Warehouse was located on the northwest corner of Main and Great Jones Streets, with Lea, Warren, and Pope as proprietors. After unloading their tobacco at the right side of the building, the farmers would spend the night on the second floor of the warehouse. Last used by the Norfolk and Western Railroad, it was torn down in the mid-1970's. The sketch dates back to about 1890.

Drawing courtesy of Duke Homestead Tobacco Museum

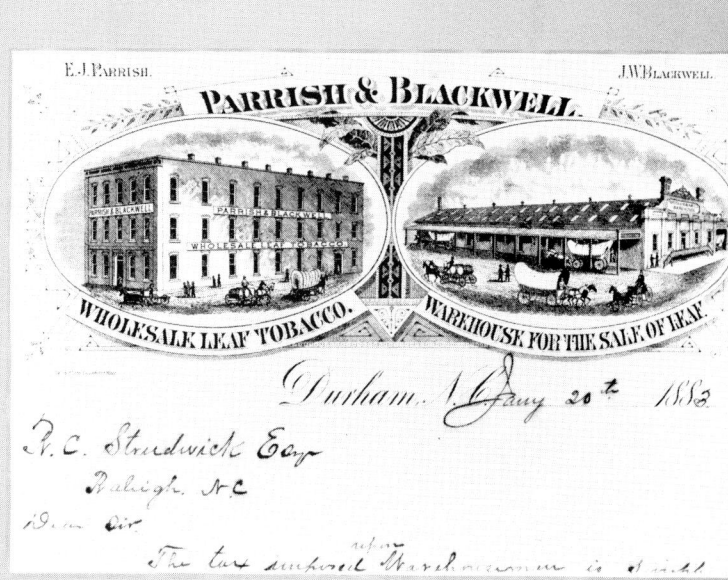

E. J. Parrish and J. W. Blackwell were involved in the sale and storage of leaf tobacco on Clay Street—later known as Parrish Street—at Mangum Street. Elaborate letterhead stationery was common. This letter was dated January 20, 1883.

Letter courtesy of State Division of Archives and History

A rolling hogshead barrel is depicted in 1953 to show how tobacco had been brought to town in former days. Note that the bull in the Bull Durham sign faces to the right; if one were looking to the north, the bull would be facing east. This was done purposely so that the bull held its head in the direction of the "older world," and it was the form of Bull Durham's original trademarks. In later days, the company turned its symbol around to face expanding America.

Photograph courtesy of Duke University Manuscript Department

The Durham Bull is shown on this pack of hand-rolled cigarettes.

Photograph courtesy of Duke University Manuscript Department

The Bull Durham plant. The factory added the right third of the building as the company expanded. The addition took the place of the Durham Warehouse of H. A. Reams, where the first tobacco auction was held. The white building to the right behind the factory is the old Morehead School, Durham's first publicly owned school, later gutted by fire and torn down.

Photograph courtesy of Duke University Manuscript Department

J. W. Blackwell.

Photograph courtesy of Duke University Manuscript Department

Advertising Blackwell's "Bull Durham Smoking Tobacco." The Durham Bull was known throughout the world in the 1870's and 1880's, largely due to the advertising efforts of Julian S. Carr. The baseball term "bullpen" originated with a painting of the Durham bull in the area where the pitcher warmed up.

Courtesy of Duke Homestead Tobacco Museum

Nick Worchester, 62, an American Indian, pauses along an Ada, Oklahoma, street, to roll a Bull Durham cigarette on May 26, 1977.

Photograph courtesy of Wide World Photos

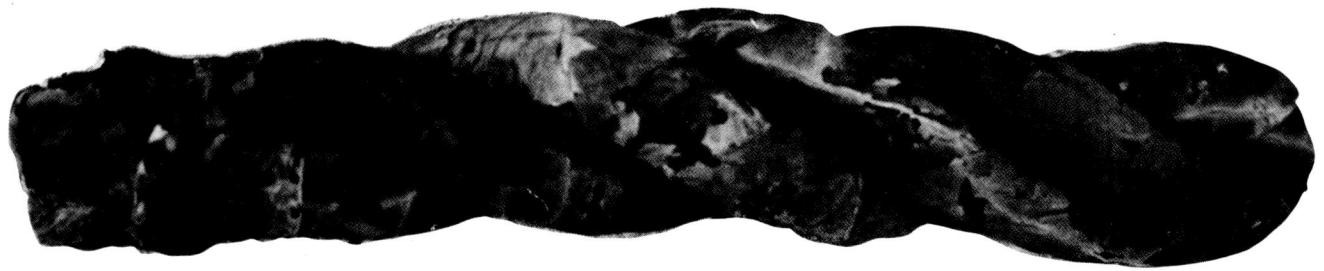

The twist was a handy way to store and carry tobacco. Bits were chopped off to be smoked in pipes or chewed.

Courtesy of Duke University Manuscript Department, photograph by Frank A. Kostyu

J. T. Mallory, from an engraving about 1895. The Mallory Company made the popular small cigar known as cheroots.

Photograph from Handbook of Durham *by Educator Company, 1895*

Mr. and Mrs. J. M. Whitted received this silver chalice and urn from William T. Blackwell upon their marriage, in August, 1882. The photo was taken in the fall of 1977 at the home of Mrs. Ella Whitted Parks.

Photograph by Frank A. Kostyu

A Day on the Tobacco Market

The tobacco market has been a significant part of Durham's history and economy. Prior to 1865, the closest tobacco market was in Danville, Virginia. It was not until May 18, 1871, that the first tobacco auction was held in Durham. The first leaf was bought by William T. Blackwell; E. J. Parrish was the auctioneer. Warehouses sprang up in what is now the downtown area as local citizens and outsiders realized the vast economic opportunities.

Regardless of the season, tobacco farmers brought their crops by the wagonload to Durham. Since it would sometimes take several days to sell their product, the farmers brought food, eating utensils, and extra clothing. The various warehouses supplied rooms for their patrons. The floors were hard, but the rooms provided a haven for sleep. When enough tobacco was on hand, farmers, buyers, auctioneers, and anyone else interested were summoned to the warehouse by a man blowing on a horn. The influx of people and money led to the expanding financial foundation of the community.

The photos that follow take the reader back to mid-November 1939. Howard W. Odum, a southern regional sociologist from Chapel Hill, made a detailed survey of the Durham tobacco market.

One of the important warehouses was owned by S. T. Mangum, a prominent name in Durham, and A. J. Rogers. Because of the advent of World War II, sales were not conducted in the usual manner. There was a "first sale" of the day and even a "second." The warehouses were so full that the sales lasted all day: the day usually began at 9 a.m., the lunch hour was 12:30 to 1:30, and the sales closed at 4 p.m. The Mangum warehouse had the welcome sign out for the farmers and provided a cafe for ladies and gents. Atlantic Beer-Ale was 10 cents.

Photograph courtesy of Southern Historical Collection, University of North Carolina, The Howard Washington Odum Collection

Tired tobacco farmers take a break in a sleeping room of a warehouse.

Photograph courtesy of Southern Historical Collection, University of North Carolina, Howard Washington Odum Collection

A lunchstand in a tobacco warehouse. Notice the hands of tobacco in the foreground.

Photograph courtesy of Southern Historical Collection, University of North Carolina, The Howard Washington Odum Collection

Lunch hour was a time for discussion; topics might include the weather, the events of the day, or the price of tobacco. Note the prices posted for some of the more popular items.

Photograph courtesy of Southern Historical Collection, University of North Carolina, The Howard Washington Odum Collection

A farmer riding his mule bareback stops to talk to a fellow farmer who is offering his automobile for sale—$40 is the asking price. The equestrian probably wants to know about miles per gallon, year and make, and whether the owner might be interested in a mule as a trade-in.

Photograph courtesy of Southern Historical Collection, University of North Carolina, The Howard Washington Odum Collection

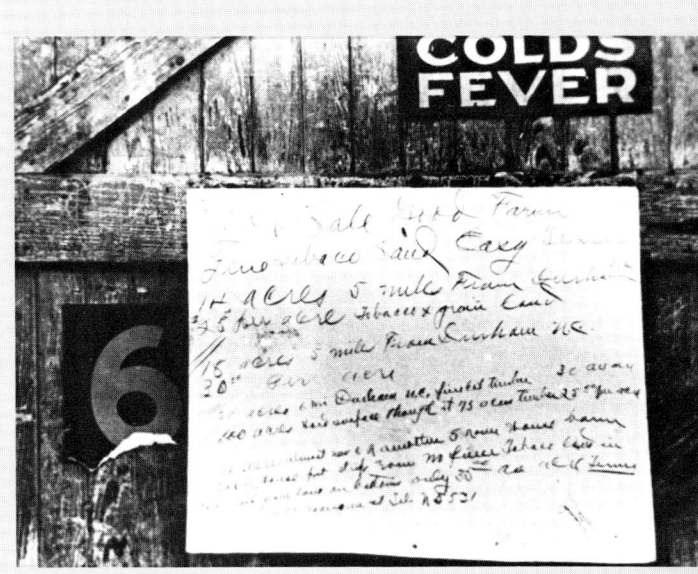

At the tobacco sales, announcements were as common as those now found on bulletin boards in supermarkets. Here the real estate dealer at 400 Mangum Street, telephone N5531, has property for sale: 14 acres of fine tobacco land, five miles from Durham, can be purchased for $25 per acre.

Photograph courtesy of Southern Historical Collection, University of North Carolina, The Howard Washington Odum Collection

Cars, trailers, and trucks, heavily laden with tobacco, line up at the Banner Warehouse.

Photograph courtesy of Southern Historical Collection, University of North Carolina, The Howard Washington Odum Collection

Mr. Wilkins looks at his trailer loaded with tobacco which is to be auctioned off at the warehouse. Tied to the top of his load is a bicycle which he brought into town to be repaired.

Photograph courtesy of Southern Historical Collection, University of North Carolina, The Howard Washington Odum Collection

Almost everyone—patent medicine salesmen, itinerant "foot doctors," photographers—was after the tobacco farmer's dollar. Pictured here is an appliance store, Huntley Stockton-Hill Co., making its pitch—a free turkey with each range and (note the decrease in size of the words "up to") a $10 allowance for the old stove.

Photograph courtesy of Southern Historical Collection, University of North Carolina, The Howard Washington Odum Collection

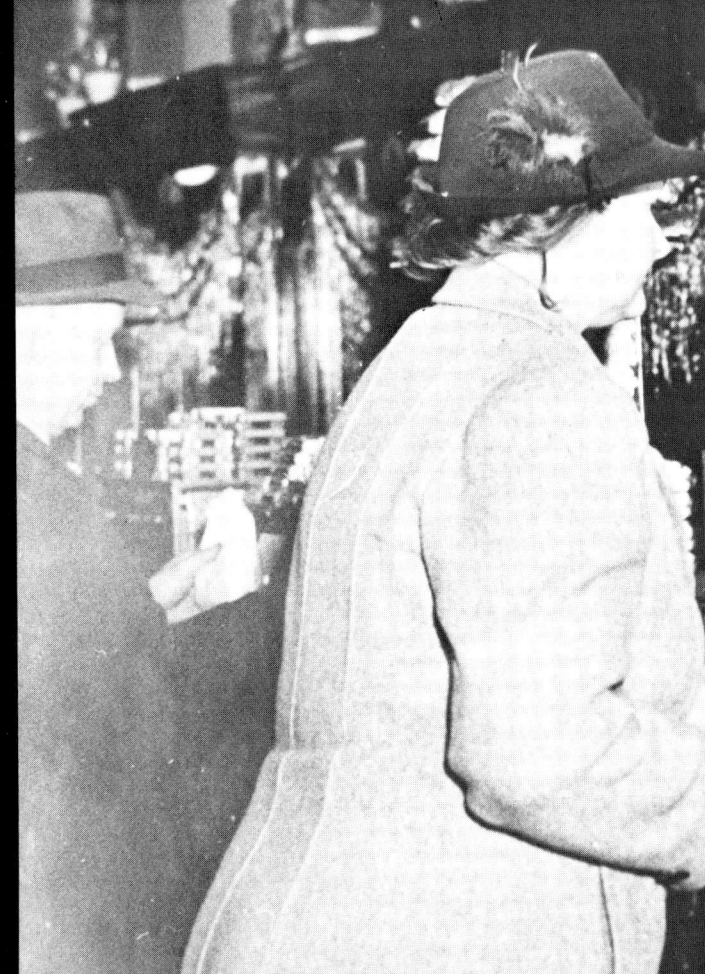

A tobacco farmer's wife celebrates the sale of her family's tobacco. What a great treat to have a box of chocolate-covered cherries from the nearest drug store!

Photograph courtesy of Southern Historical Collection, University of North Carolina, The Howard Washington Odum Collection

A tobacco auctioneer who bet on the University of North Carolina football team and lost pays off his wager by pushing a warehouseman from the tobacco warehouse to the Durham courthouse. The game was played on Saturday, November 18, 1939; the score was Duke, 13; UNC, 3.

Photograph courtesy of Southern Historical Collection, University of North Carolina The Howard Washington Odum Collection

The Commonwealth Cotton Manufacturing Company was incorporated June 1, 1890, but operations did not start on a full scale until January 1, 1893. The company, with Brodie Duke as president and V. Ballard as treasurer, made white and colored yarn and hosiery.

Photograph courtesy of Wyatt T. Dixon

At the turn of the century, a group of prominent Durham citizens gathered in Duke, North Carolina, to consider the building of a textile mill. In the first row, left to right, are: Benjamin Duke, Washington Duke, James B. Duke, two unidentified persons, J. S. Cobb, and J. C. Angier. In the back row are: A. G. Carr, W. A. Erwin, J. E. Stagg, Frank Tate, E. S. Yarborough, Colonel Lemon, and Frank L. Fuller.

The small town in Harnett County was named Duke in 1903 at the insistence of W. A. Erwin, manager of the Duke mill interests. To avoid the confusion associated with renaming Trinity College as Duke University in Durham, President William P. Few in November, 1925, requested a change in the small town's name. Thereafter, it has been called Erwin, North Carolina.

Photograph courtesy of Duke University Manuscript Department

Erwin Cotton Mills at West Main and Ninth Streets was opened in 1893. Financed by the Duke tobacco fortunes, William A. Erwin managed this and other mills with deft managerial skills. The mills eventually became among the nation's largest manufacturers of denim. Erwin was instrumental in prohibiting under-age children from working in the mills, in addition to reducing the working-day hours from 13 to 11.

Photograph courtesy of Duke University Manuscript Department

Golden Belt Manufacturing Company, owned by American Brands, is now involved in commercial printing and closely tied to the tobacco industry. It once made cloth sacks for tobacco.

Photograph courtesy of Wyatt T. Dixon

This unidentified picture is probably the interior of a sewing room in a textile mill.

Photograph courtesy of Durham Chamber of Commerce

Contemporary shots of Duke Knitting Mills, Inc., show time has taken its toll. The building is empty and wind whistles through its shattered windows. They say the visitor can hear voices and looms from days gone by.

Photograph by Frank A. Kostyu

Duke Knitting Mill gate padlocked and bolted.

Photograph by Frank A. Kostyu

The Durham Electric Lighting Company on Peabody Street near Roxboro was organized in 1885 by Julian S. Carr, Eugene Morehead, and George W. Watts and started operations in 1886.

Photograph courtesy of Wyatt T. Dixon

In 1899 an explosion destroyed the Durham Electric Lighting Company building. Four people were injured, none seriously.

Photograph courtesy of Wyatt T. Dixon

The old gas plant, located on Gilbert Street, was erected at the turn of the century. The Durham Traction Company was to supply electricity, and the Light and Power Company was to provide gas. The cost of the plant and lines was over $200,000. Gas lights on sidewalks were a common sight at the time, and the lamplighter became a familiar figure as he turned off the gas in the morning and turned on and lit the lamps in the evening.

Photograph courtesy of Wyatt T. Dixon

The Durham Light and Power Company started operations 1900-01. Along with the Durham Traction Company, it received franchises from Durham to supply limited lighting and electric power. Both companies supplied ice as one of their services.

Photograph courtesy of Wyatt T. Dixon

Back in 1914 the ice wagon was a childhood delight. As it stopped, children would gather to grab chips of ice and suck the cooling treat. If the ice man was in a good mood, he might purposely see that a few extra chips fell from the block. Ice, cut from rivers up north in the winter months, was shipped in freight carlots covered with thick layers of sawdust. A. A. Holder was one of the first ice dealers in Durham.

Photograph courtesy of Wyatt T. Dixon

Lake Michie was built in 1924 through 1926 and named after one of Durham's most prominent citizens, the first superintendent of the water works. The new facilities replaced the old pump station on the Eno River which dated back to 1887. Captain Jack C. Michie (1863-1939) was instrumental in getting a state law passed for the protection of water sheds and a state laboratory established to test the water in cities of North Carolina.

The first water meter in Durham was installed on June 24, 1887 in the home of W. A. Guthrie on the northeast corner of Main and Queen Streets.

Photograph by Frank A. Kostyu from Handbook of Durham, *1895*

Plaque at Lake Michie.

Photograph courtesy of Wyatt T. Dixon

Lake Michie under construction. Located north of Durham, it has been an asset to the town for many years, not only as a vital water supply, but also as a source of contentment to many a fisherman. During the dry summers of 1976 and 1977, the reservoir also provided water for Chapel Hill.

Photograph courtesy of Wyatt T. Dixon

Lake Michie after completion.

Photograph courtesy of Wyatt T. Dixon

The Morehead Bank is shown at the left, next to Angier's General Store, located at what is now the northwest corner of Main and Mangum Street.

Photograph courtesy of Wyatt T. Dixon

Eugene Morehead, son of a former governor of North Carolina, Governor John M. Morehead, came to Durham in 1878 and within six months had organized the town's first bank. After Morehead's death in 1889, the bank was reorganized as the Morehead Banking company.

Photograph courtesy of Wyatt T. Dixon

In 1905, the Morehead Bank was again reorganized as the Citizens National Bank, with Benjamin Duke as president. Southgate and Son Insurance Company was located on the second floor of this building. The Citizens National Bank of Durham and Roxboro merged with the Durham Bank and Trust Company in 1959, and with the University National Bank in Chapel Hill in 1961, to form the Central Carolina Bank and Trust Company.

Photograph courtesy of Duke University Manuscript Department

In 1887 the Fidelity Savings and Trust Company was organized and began business in 1888. Among the founders were Washington Duke, George W. Watts, Benjamin N. Duke, and M. A. Angier. The company's purpose was to do business as a savings bank, but it expanded into a commercial bank. When capitalization was increased in 1889, the institution changed its name to Fidelity Bank. A large amount of the Dukes' money went into the bank, and Benjamin Duke and George Watts each served as president for several years. The quarters were rented in a building near Main and Corcoran Streets.

The Fidelity was later absorbed by the Wachovia Bank, shown here occupying the Geer Building on the northeast corner of Main and Corcoran Streets. The Geer Building, constructed after the devastating

The First National Bank, chartered in November, 1887, originally had its headquarters at Main and Church Streets. Shown here is the bank's second building, located on the southeast corner of Main and Corcoran Streets, which was occupied from 1893 to 1914. Today the North Carolina National Bank Building occupies the site.

Photograph courtesy of Wyatt T. Dixon

The North Carolina National Bank is located at the southeast corner of East Main and Corcoran Streets. The large vertical sign has been removed and the structure is being restored to its original 1914 exterior.

Photograph courtesy of Durham Chamber of Commerce

fire of 1914 and modelled on a Florentine palace, was named for Fred C. Geer, a Durham philanthropist in the early part of this century. After Wachovia moved its quarters to its new building on the southwest corner of Main and Corcoran, the Geer Building was torn down.

Photograph courtesy of Durham Chamber of Commerce

The North Carolina Mutual Life Insurance Company is the largest predominantly black-managed financial institution in the United States. The 12-story landmark at the southeast corner of Duke and Chapel Hill Streets is a proud monument to the doctrine of self-help through commercial enterprise.

The North Carolina Mutual had its philosophical roots in the late eighteenth century with the Free African Society, which emphasized self-help, racial solidarity, and moral uplift as an effort to respond to the conditions of a hostile white environment. Another milestone in the development of black enterprise was the organization of the Grand United Order of the True Reformers in 1881 in Richmond, Virginia, by William Washington Browne. A black mutual benefit society that Browne expanded to include an insurance company and, among other things, the first all-black bank, the True Reformers boasted 100,000 members by 1900, but was doomed by overexpansion in 1910. One member of the True Reformers, John Merrick, joined in 1883 with Durham leaders to form the Royal Knights of King David, a fraternal organization which died early as a result of inadequate rates due to a lack of reliable information on black mortality. Merrick, however, gained the essential background to establish and succeed with the North Carolina Mutual.

The North Carolina Mutual and Provident Association was organized October 20, 1898, with John Merrick generally regarded as the founder. Dr. Aaron McDuffie Moore, Durham's first black physician, together with D. T. Watson, James E. Shepard, P. W. Dawkins, E. A. Johnson, and W. G. Pearson, were a part of the early organization. After incorporation by the General Assembly of the State of North Carolina on February 28, 1899, the company commenced business on April 1, 1899. Its motto was "Merciful to All," with the purpose of providing "relief to the widows and orphans, of the sick, to those injured by accident, and for the burial of the dead."

The premium receipts from April 1, 1899, to December 31, 1899, came to $672.45. After subtracting the commissions of 14 part-time agents and incidental expenses, the net sum remaining was $393.95, hardly an auspicious beginning! In the first six months of 1900, the number of sick claims increased. The bleak financial outlook led all the organizers except Merrick and Moore to resign. Charles Clinton Spaulding, a local part-time agent and nephew of Dr. Moore, was appointed general manager on July 1, 1900. Merrick, Moore, and Spaulding thus formed the management team, sometimes known as the Triumvirate, and served as the board of directors until January, 1911.

The enthusiasm, optimism, and good business sense of Spaulding, along with the financial support of Merrick and Moore, enabled the company to turn the financial corner in 1902, and the business began to pay for itself. Merrick's association with white business leaders resulted in sound investment opportunities and timely loans that increased the financial solidarity of the N. C. Mutual. The company changed its name to the North Carolina Mutual Life Insurance Company in 1919.

After the deaths of Merrick in 1919 and Moore in 1923, C. C. Spaulding assumed the reins of the presidency. During his tenure of more than 29 years, the North Carolina Mutual continued its growth and prosperity.

Under subsequent presidents W. J. Kennedy, Jr. (1952-1958), Asa T. Spaulding (1958-1967), Joseph W. Goodloe (1968-1972), and W. J. Kennedy, III, (1972-   ), the North Carolina Mutual Life Insurance Company has continued to promote community and national service. In 1977 the assets were nearly 160 million dollars; over three billion dollars in insurance were in force. The company ranks 150th in both categories among more than 1,700 life insurance companies licensed to operate in the United States.

The Triumvirate: John Merrick (1859-1919), left, owned six barber shops and a real estate business. He was elected first president of the Association, (1899-1919).

Dr. Aaron M. Moore (1863-1923), center, was the first black physician to practice in Durham. Besides his major role in the development of North Carolina Mutual, Dr. Moore founded Lincoln Hospital in 1901 and what is now the Stanford L. Warren Library in 1913. He served as president of the North Carolina Mutual from 1919 to 1923.

Charles Clinton Spaulding (1874-1952), right, was appointed general manager of the Association on July 1, 1900. His dynamic leadership earned him the presidency from 1923 to 1952. He became a national figure in black enterprise and civil rights.

Photograph courtesy of North Carolina Mutual Life Insurance Company

The office of the infant insurance company was in a section of Dr. Moore's office. Shown here are C. C. Spaulding and Dora Whitted, his clerk, in the second office at 121½ East Main Street. The office remained here until 1905, when the North Carolina Mutual moved into its first home office building.

Photograph courtesy of North Carolina Mutual Life Insurance Company

The first home office building, pictured here in January 1, 1906, was located on West Parrish Street. The *Durham Daily Sun* wrote: "This is indeed a remarkable record for the endeavors of Negroes, and the *Sun* gives it to the world what they are doing in Durham, with very great pleasure." This building was demolished in 1920 to make way for the construction of a building with more space to handle the expanding business. The home office remained on West Parrish Street until 1966, when the office on Chapel Hill Street was occupied.

Photograph courtesy of North Carolina Mutual Life Insurance Company

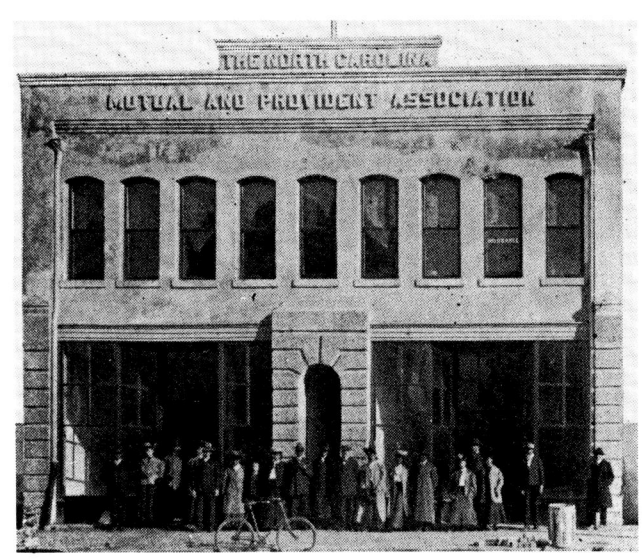

Mechanics and Farmers Bank, shown in the 1930's, shared the second home office building of North Carolina Mutual. The combined assets of bank and insurance company elicited the proclamation that Parrish Street was the Black Wall Street of America.

Photograph courtesy of North Carolina Mutual Life Insurance Company

Charles Clinton Spaulding was a salesman as well as general manager of the Association. Spaulding used this circa 1905 picture on the face of postcards as a form of advertising.

Photograph courtesy of North Carolina Mutual Life Insurance Company

First office of the North Carolina Mutual and Provident Association of Durham, in a photograph probably taken at the beginning of the present century.

Photograph courtesy of Duke University Manuscript Department

The North Carolina Mutual Life Insurance Building at the southeast corner of West Chapel Hill Street and South Duke Street.

Photograph by Frank A. Kostyu

The S. S. John Merrick was launched on Sunday, July 11, 1943. The 10,500 ton Liberty Ship was the 113th to be launched by the North Carolina Shipbuilding Company. Governor J. Melville Broughton said in the dedication address: "....it is fervently hoped that the life and character of this great man may be brought freshly to the minds of both races in North Carolina; that in the light of his wholesome philosophy and successful career we may find a path of harmony, success, victory, and peace, through mutual respect and honest cooperation."

Photograph courtesy of North Carolina Mutual Life Insurance Company

Booker T. Washington visited the North Carolina Mutual Life Insurance Company in Durham in 1910. Mr. Washington is sixth from the left in the second row. John Merrick is to his left. C. C. Spaulding is fourth from the left in the first row.

Washington had been touring a number of cities and towns in North Carolina to praise the industrial progress of blacks. The climax of his tour was Durham, where the North Carolina Mutual and Provident Association clearly demonstrated his philosophy of self-help through economic enterprise. He later wrote that "of all the Southern cities I visited, I found here the sanest attitude of the white people toward the black. I never saw in a city of this size so many prosperous carpenters, brickmasons, blacksmiths, wheelwrights, cotton mill operatives, and tobacco factory workers among the Negroes."

Photograph courtesy of North Carolina Mutual Life Insurance Company

On April 2, 1966, the new home office of the North Carolina Mutual Life Insurance Company was dedicated. Many national figures were in attendance, among them the late Vice President Hubert H. Humphrey, who gave the dedication address. Mr. Humphrey is shown here accepting a gift from Asa T. Spaulding. Mrs. Muriel Humphrey is in the left background.

Said Mr. Humphrey: "History teaches us that the great revolutions aren't started by people who are utterly down and out—without hope and vision. They take place when people begin to live a little better—and when they see how much yet remains to be achieved. I say these demands and this striving will not and cannot end until all Negroes enjoy the full rights and privileges and opportunities of other American citizens, both in law and in fact."

Asa T. Spaulding, North Carolina Mutual president from 1958 to 1967, was the first professionally trained black actuary in this country. After coming to North Carolina Mutual in January, 1933, he was instrumental in establishing continued growth after the Depression years.

Photograph courtesy of North Carolina Mutual Life Insurance Company

In the town of Hillsborough in 1872, a shingle hung on the door of a small one-story frame building, reading "James Southgate, Life and Fire Insurance Agent." At 41, Southgate knew what hardship was. He had no money, but a wife and four small children were dependent on him. Too poor to afford a buggy, he stored his insurance applications and policies, along with a quill pen and a bottle of ink, in his saddlebags and took to the road.

In 1876 Durham was showing a great deal of activity, especially due to the growth of the tobacco industry, so James Southgate cast his lot with the 600 citizens of the town. He moved his desk, two chairs, and two J. and P. Coats spool cabinets together with his shingle and announced to Durham that he was an agent for life and fire insurance.

J. Southgate and Son Insurance agency is one of the oldest in the county and is the oldest in North Carolina still controlled by a direct descendant of the founder. According to Southgate Jones, Jr., it is also the oldest business firm in Durham. The first company represented by James Southgate was Seaboard Fire Insurance Company of Virginia.

Photograph courtesy of Southgate Jones, Jr.

Mr. and Mrs. S. A. Thaxton on the lot where Southgate Jones' home once stood on West Chapel Hill Street. The Downtowner Motor Inn now occupies the site.

Photograph courtesy of Wyatt T. Dixon

Home Security Life Insurance Company was organized by three leading Durham citizens—John Sprunt Hill, A. M. Moize, and his brother E. N. Moize—on May 30, 1916. Along with its $661,544 insurance in force written during the first 6½ months of operation, the fledgling firm realized $19,414 in premiums, $1,074 in interest and benefits of $3,743 paid to policy-holders and beneficiaries. At the end of 1977, over two billion dollars of life insurance were in force. The company ranks in the top fifteen percent of the more than 1,700 life insurance companies in the United States on the basis of insurance in force. Home Security conducts operations through 34 district offices, mostly in the southeastern United States; it has 900 employees, including a sales force of 650.

The first home of the insurance company was the Trust Building. Having outgrown the cramped quarters there, the company moved to the second floor of the Temple Building, shown here, at the northwest corner of Main and Market Streets. Now used by the Guaranty State Bank, it was erected in 1909.

Photograph by Frank A. Kostyu

In 1936 Home Security Life moved to the sixth floor of the Hill Building. Continual growth necessitated a new home, shown here, for which ground was broken on February 21, 1957, by one of the original founders, John Sprunt Hill. In 1973 Home Security Life became an affiliate company of the Capital Holding Corporation of Louisville, Kentucky. Arthur W. Clark was elected chairman of the board and president in 1975, the same year in which Palmetto State Life Insurance of Columbia, South Carolina, merged with Home Security Life. Earlier, two other companies had likewise merged, Capital Life Insurance Company of Raleigh (1931) and Greensboro Life Insurance Company (1932). Significantly, with the latter merger came Bascom Baynes, under whose presidency the company experienced a healthy growth.

*Photograph by Walter E. Shackelford,
courtesy of Home Security Life Insurance Company*

S. R. Carrington's Bar was a popular place in the 1880's.

Photograph courtesy of Duke University Manuscript Department

Archie Gurganus sold fruit and soft drinks in front of his house at Main near Morris Street. There were several shops like this in the downtown area around 1915.

Photograph courtesy of Wyatt T. Dixon

Saloons did a thriving business in Durham prior to 1902, when local voters opted for prohibition. One such saloon used to stand at the northwest corner of Mangum and Peabody Streets. The old Durham Hosiery Mill where silk hosiery was made is at the rear.

Photograph courtesy of Wyatt T. Dixon

Located at the southwest corner of Main and Mangum Streets, the John L. Markham Cash Store was the first business firm to operate from a brick structure in Durham. Although the construction date is not known, the first meeting of the Board of County Commissioners, after the formation of Durham County, was held on the second floor on May 2, 1881.

Photograph courtesy of Wyatt T. Dixon

C. E. King, fifth from left, in his drug store at the northwest corner of Main and Mangum. Today, the counter stools are considered antiques.

Photograph courtesy of Wyatt T. Dixon

In the depression of 1930, 400 farmers with $2,400 in capital organized Farmers Exchange for the purpose of developing good markets for what they produced on their farms and lowering their costs of feed, seed, fertilizer, and farm supplies.

Forty-three years later, 6,000 farmers from Durham, Orange, Chatham, Granville, and Person Counties owned and operated Central Carolina Farmers at 301 Gilbert Street. These farmers' assets reached 16.2 million dollars invested in land, buildings, and equipment. Each year, after interest is paid to the farmer on the stock he owns in the Exchange, the remaining profits derived from the operations of the organization are refunded to the patron who furnished the marketing and purchasing volume.

Photograph by Joel A. Kostyu

Staff photo of H. E. Seeman Steam Printery, taken in 1895. Left to right, standing: Tom Whitaker, Belfield Laws, unidentified, John B. Wilburn, Newton Pendergraph, Claud Allison; seated: H. E. Seeman, Henry Chamberlain. Not in photo: George Lougee, Louis Chamberlain. A notation made on the back of the photo in February, 1955, states, "The first person is not Tom but Charlie Whitaker."

Photograph courtesy of Seeman Printery

Four Jourdan Transfer trucks are loaded with tile and ready to go in this photograph taken in the 1930's. It could have been a rough ride to their destination on those solid rubber tires. The company was founded by Stanislaus Jourdan, a native of France who settled in Durham about 1887 and started his hauling business with a horse and wagon.

Photograph courtesy of Duke University Manuscript Department

The Research Triangle Park is set in the geographic triangle formed by Duke University, the University of North Carolina, and North Carolina State University. All the present buildings in the park are located in Durham County. In this area there are more Ph.D.s in relation to the population than in any other part of the nation. The Burroughs-Wellcome Building, shown here, has become a symbol of the progress and future of the park.

Photograph by Frank A. Kostyu

The name of T. O. Sharp was associated with the monument business in Durham for many years. The picture was taken in 1910 and shows the business located at the Chapel Hill Street railroad crossing prior to the construction of the underpass in the late 1920's. In the right background across the tracks is the American Tobacco Company. Behind Sharp's business is the Budd-Piper Roofing Company.

Photograph courtesy of Wyatt T. Dixon

The tracks of the North Carolina Railroad passed near the Duke tobacco factory.

Drawing courtesy of Duke University Manuscript Department

TRANSPORTATION

Durham grew as opportunities abounded in the tobacco-based economy, and improved transportation was essential to take full advantage of the growth potential. The Richmond and Danville Railroad, which had the lease to the old North Carolina Railroad track, had a monopolistic hold on freight and passenger service in the 1870's. With unregulated freight charges and generally poor service, the local industrialists sought ways to increase the competition. Several small lines connecting Durham and neighboring cities were established: The Lynchburg and Durham, the Durham and Clarksville, the Durham and Northern, and the Durham and Southern. A multitude of legal battles and actual physical violence ensued over right-of-ways when depots and terminals of the new lines had to be located as much as a mile away from Durham's center, especially inconvenient for the large tobacco factories.

The townspeople finally took matters into their own hands. The town council authorized the Durham and Northern Railroad to run its track up Peabody Street to the eastern end of the W. Duke, Sons, and Company tobacco factory. About midnight on Monday, April 9, 1889, townspeople, under the supervision of the Durham and Northern Railroad engineers, started building the extension that was within the right-of-way of the Richmond and Danville Railroad. At daybreak, the line was completed to Corcoran Street. The Richmond and Danville Railroad then had the entire number of workmen arrested for forcible trespassing. When the warrants were dismissed, work resumed, and by early Wednesday morning, the Durham and Northern track was completed to the Duke Factory. About 11 a.m. the same day, Richmond and Danville workmen arrived and managed to destroy about 100 feet of the new track before being persuaded by the police to desist. The extension, known as the "Moonlight Railroad," was subsequently completed and put into service.

Later railroad developments were not nearly so exciting and dramatic as during the 1880's and 1890's. Service to Charlotte and South Carolina was established, and later the Cape Fear and Northern was extended to Durham. No other city in the state had such a variety of railway facilities. In the 1970's, only freight service is available.

The Durham Street Railway Company was organized in 1885 for the purpose of operating a

Covered wagons go to mill. This Roxboro Road bridge was washed away in a 1908 flood.

Photograph courtesy of Margaret Nygard

street railway system. An exclusive 15-year franchise, received in 1887, permitted either mule- or horse-drawn rail cars. In 1891 the company reorganized under the management of the Durham Consolidated Land and Improvement Company in an effort to secure a firmer financial base. This company and the city agreed on steam as the source of power for the cars; they felt it was less dangerous than electricity. The eventual downfall of the venture was mostly the result of the trackage being six to eight inches above the rock and earth streets, causing problems for other modes of traffic.

The franchise of the Durham Street Railway Company was purchased by the Durham Traction Company in 1901. Since the Traction Company, organized by Richard H. Wright, Sr., J. S. Manning, H. A. Foushee, and others, was involved in the production of electricity, this source of power was deemed more acceptable at that time.

In 1912 the control went to the H. L. Doharty Company, and the name of the branch in Durham was changed to Durham Public Service Company. Its greatest business was retailing electric lights and manufacturing ice.

Not many young people will remember the "iron horse" of the early twentieth century. Two of them are depicted here in Durham's Union Station. Mail and passengers aboard the train were ready to highball along the Atlantic seaboard that seemed too far away for many to comprehend.

Postcard courtesy of Stephen Massengill

This is the first Seaboard train to run from Henderson to Durham, about 1888. The trainmen were Joe R. Renn, conductor; Mike Tie, engineer; and J. F. Alston, fireman.

Photograph courtesy of Wyatt T. Dixon

Durham's contingent of volunteers on the first leg of a journey to fight in the Spanish-American War in May, 1898. The train stands beside the little passenger depot. In the upper right is the Hotel Carrolina. The war had ended by the time the men had reached Cuba.

The passengers had to put up with soot and dust as part of the trip. Today's railroad hobbyists consider it a privilege to ride these antiques of an era rapidly passing with time.

Photograph courtesy of Wyatt T. Dixon

Old passenger station across railroad from the American Tobacco Company.

Photograph courtesy of Wyatt T. Dixon

The Durham and Northern Railroad was incorporated by a special act of the state legislature on February 2, 1887, to construct a rail line and operate a railroad. The depot on Peabody Street was used for both freight and passengers. Each railroad company had its own station. The Durham and Northern Railroad was sold to the Seaboard Air Line on September 13, 1903. The restrooms in the station were labeled "white" and "colored" from the bygone era of segregation.

Photograph courtesy of Wyatt T. Dixon

The horse-drawn supply wagon may not have given the passenger the smooth ride of today's automobile, but it did get him where he wanted to go. The men here were visiting Green Brothers at 108 North Mangum Street.

Photograph courtesy of Wyatt T. Dixon

Sarah P. Duke is shown with her two children in a horse-drawn carriage, about 1890.

Photograph courtesy of Duke University Manuscript Department

A horse-drawn carriage and a trolley at the corner of Main and Corcoran Streets. In the background are the old Post Office and the Trust Building.

Photograph courtesy of Wyatt T. Dixon

From the old trolley car barns, the buses are ready to roll.

Photograph courtesy of Wyatt T. Dixon

Members of the trolley company in the 1920's. In the center is the Lakewood Park trolley.

Photograph courtesy of Wyatt T. Dixon

The bicycle was a popular form of entertainment as well as a useful mode of transportation at the end of the nineteenth century. Two-wheelers such as these could be rented for ten cents per hour at a place like B. L. Duke and Company's furniture store. The expressions on the men's faces suggest that their bikes were a badge of courage.

Photograph courtesy of Wyatt T. Dixon

Directing traffic is Charles Williams Edwards, Jr., while Charles, Sr., stands by. Photograph was taken in the back yard at 406 Buchanan Boulevard around 1920. Charles, Sr., was a physicist who taught at Trinity College and Duke University for 46 years. He died in 1955 at age 81.

Charles, Jr., now farms and operates an apple orchard in Junaluska. The homeplace on Buchanan is now occupied by the Daniel Kramer Edwards family.

Photograph courtesy of Jane Edwards

The mule car was replaced in 1902 by electric trolleys which ran from Mangum at Trinity to Lakewood Park and from East to West Durham. The trolleys were a welcome form of mass transit; however, like all forms of transportation, they were not without problems. When the trolley first began operations, there was a baseball game in the George Lyon ballpark. After the game, the fans rushed aboard the new trolley cars. Unfortunately, the power failed. Soon the cars began moving, but for a second time the power failed. Many red faces could be seen when horses were called on to pull the cars back to the barn. In 1930, trolley service was supplemented by motor buses, and the last trolley was discarded in 1932. The tracks are now covered by pavement.

Photograph courtesy of Wyatt T. Dixon

Automobiles line up in Durham for the annual big game between Duke and the University of North Carolina on November 18, 1939. Duke won: 13-3. Finding a parking spot for the games continues to be a problem.

Photographs courtesy of Southern Historical Collection, University of North Carolina, The Howard Washington Odum Collection

Increasing expansion and modernization have paralleled the growth of the Research Triangle area which the Raleigh-Durham Airport serves. This photograph was taken at 5 p.m. on April 9, 1950.

Photograph courtesy of Raleigh-Durham Airport Authority

EDUCATION

Durham's first public school was located in a two-story rented building known as Wright's Factory, on the north side of Main Street adjacent to what is now the Liggett-Myers Tobacco Factory. It opened its doors on September 4, 1882, with E. W. Kennedy as superintendent and with an enrollment of some 308 students. Eugene Morehead, J. B. Whitaker, and Bartholomew Fuller made up the first Board of Education. Though fears that the school would be obliged to close were voiced, it nevertheless remained at this same location for about ten years.

To keep the school running and to raise money for a city-owned school, taxes were levied. Objecting to the raising of school taxes, A. M. Rigsbee took the case to the Supreme Court of North Carolina, which decided that the law establishing the Durham Graded School was unconstitutional largely because of racial discrimination. W. T. Blackwell emphatically declared that he would rather see all the factories in town close down than to allow the school's collapse. He rallied other citizens to meet the salaries and school expenses until a new law could be enacted that would conform to the constitution, and residents could once more vote taxes for the education of Durham's youngsters. The Graded School continued as a private school for the school year of 1886-87 until a new law was indeed enacted.

Photograph courtesy of Wyatt T. Dixon

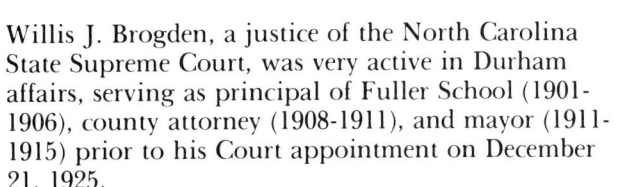

Morehead School on Jackson Street welcomed students in the fall of 1892, and Wright's Factory was no longer in use.

Photograph courtesy of Wyatt T. Dixon

Willis J. Brogden, a justice of the North Carolina State Supreme Court, was very active in Durham affairs, serving as principal of Fuller School (1901-1906), county attorney (1908-1911), and mayor (1911-1915) prior to his Court appointment on December 21, 1925.

Portrait courtesy of First Baptist Church, photograph by Joel A. Kostyu

Durham High School, 1942. Brodie Duke's house stood near the school site on Duke Street.

Postcard courtesy of Stephen Massengill

The Fuller School, a grade school, was the oldest in the city from the standpoint of the physical plant. Note the gas street light. E. J. Green was the first principal of Fuller School. Willis J. Brogden, later a member of the State Supreme Court, also served as principal. The building was constructed on the northwest corner of Chapel Hill and Cleveland Streets in 1897 and burned on March 13, 1937. From a stereoscopic photograph.

Photograph courtesy of Blackwell Brogden

Trinity Park School, a college preparatory school, opened its doors September 11, 1898, with an enrollment of 45 students. J. F. Bevins was the headmaster of this school, which was associated with Trinity College (John C. Kilgo, president). Students and faculty had access to the college library, gymnasium, and lectures. It closed in 1922 with F. S. Aldridge as the last headmaster. The June, 1904, *Park School Gazette,* a publication of the school, adds an interesting note: "The school is not in the city, but on the north side, and has a view of a wide range of open country. This is an advantage in many ways, especially in the freedom for exercise that it gives and the freedom from the poisoned atmosphere in the crowded city."

Photograph courtesy of Duke University Archives

The first high school building was constructed on the Morris Street property in 1906. Previously, the Morehead School had housed both elementary and high school students. The property was purchased around 1925 by the city to be used as its city hall. The dome was removed. The building was abandoned in 1977 when the city occupied its new building at City Hall Plaza. Older Durham graduates can remember when the boys had to enter the left side of the building and the girls on the right. The classrooms were segregated by sex. Even at recess, a fence separated the boys from the girls! Detention resulted if a boy was caught looking through the fence.

Photograph courtesy of Stephen Massengill

Trinity College & Duke University

Trinity College, forerunner of Duke University, had its roots in Randolph County where, in 1838, a group of Methodists and Quakers established Union Institute, which met in a one-room log building. In 1851 it became Normal College, and in 1858 it was turned over to the Methodist denomination and chartered as Trinity College.

The little Methodist school was in need of funds and anticipated that moving the school to a city would be important for its future development. In May, 1889, under the leadership of its president John Franklin Crowell, a search was begun for another site.

At first, an offer from Raleigh was accepted, but after a more generous offer, spearheaded by Washington Duke with a gift of $85,000, and Julian S. Carr, who donated Blackwell Park, an area of 62 acres, Trinity decided on Durham. Other civic-minded leaders of the city also helped convince the college that Durham should be its home. In September, 1892, Trinity College, with all of its paraphernalia packed into a single boxcar, moved to Durham, becoming its first institution of higher learning. By 1895 Trinity College had twelve professors and one instructor.

Marcus A. Geddie, a student, left, and Reverend F. S. Lane, circa 1904. Of the two arches forming the gateway to Trinity College, that on the left bears the word *Eruditio*, the other the word *Religio*. Looking through the gateway, one can see the Washington Duke Building that was built for the college with funds donated by Washington Duke. The iron gate was dismantled in 1914.

Photograph courtesy of State Division of Archives and History

Washington Duke had given $100,000 to Trinity College in 1898. Many of the students and others participated in a parade to Duke's home to show appreciation for the gift. Duke is at the upper right on the porch. Trinity College was often sustained with such gifts by Washington Duke and his son Benjamin. It was not until much later that James B. Duke became involved in the financial support of the school, but when he did, he did it in a big way, with the bequest of over 40 million dollars.

Photograph courtesy of Wyatt T. Dixon

John Franklin Crowell (1857-1931) was president of Trinity College from 1887-94. President Crowell was known as an innovator; he promoted intercollegiate football and was president during Trinity's move to Durham. A northerner and non-Methodist, Crowell left the school due to friction with the faculty.

Photograph courtesy of Duke University Archives

The Washington Duke Building, originally called Old Main, was completed and occupied in September, 1892. The collapse of the tower in August, 1891, delayed the move of Trinity College from Randolph County to Durham. The building was used for administration and as a dormitory.

Photograph courtesy of Duke University Archives

James H. Southgate, right, chairman of the board of trustees at Trinity College, was a pioneer insurance man and spokesman for the Tobacco Board of Trade and the Commonwealth Club, an organization that promoted Durham's economic development. A women's dormitory, formally opened in October, 1921, on Trinity campus, was named for him in honor of his support of the school.

John Carlisle Kilgo, left, president of Trinity College from 1894 to 1910, played an important part in sparking the continuing interest of the Duke family. Idealistic and determined, Kilgo activated an era of enthusiasm. Washington Duke was particularly taken with admiration for Kilgo's preaching. In 1910 Kilgo was elected to the Methodist episcopacy.

Photograph couresty of Duke University Archives

Julian Shakespeare Carr was born in Chapel Hill, but it was in Durham that he made his fortune in tobacco. His other financial concerns included banking and cotton manufacturing. An ardent Methodist, Carr was munificent in his philanthropies.

Historian Archibald Henderson said, "I am convinced that Julian S. Carr's greatest gift to the world was...the education of Soong Chia-chun (Charlie Soong)." In 1880, he sponsored the boy and sent him to Trinity College and Vanderbilt University in Nashville, Tennessee. Soong returned to China and became prosperous. He had three daughters and three sons. One daughter married Sun Yat-sen, first president of the Republic of China; another married Dr. H. H. Kung, minister of finance; Chiang Kai-shek, former head of the Nationalist Chinese government on Formosa, married another. One son held the position of Chinese minister to Washington. (From *Durham Morning Herald*, Sunday, May 14, 1972, by George Lougee.)

Carr donated the land for Trinity College when it was moved to Durham, and he gave the land for the town's public school. Note the flower in his lapel; it is said that Julian S. Carr was never without a flower, usually one grown in his own greenhouse.

Photograph courtesy of State Division of Archives and History

John C. Kilgo, president of Trinity College from 1894 to 1910, posts his own mail.

Photograph courtesy of Duke University Archives

In 1903 John Spencer Bassett, professor of history at Trinity College, wrote in *The South Atlantic Quarterly* an article entitled "Stirring Up the Fires of Racial Antipathy." He stated that Booker T. Washington was "...the greatest man, save General Lee, born in the South in a hundred years." Bassett's statements antagonized many Americans. The trustees and faculty of Trinity felt the great pressure of public opinion as calls for Bassett's dismissal were loud and vocal, but they did not yield. The faculty issued this statement: "This college has now the opportunity to show that her campus is one spot on Southern soil where men's minds are free....We may be in danger of losing students, perhaps of losing friends, but we are willing to risk our future standing for the great principle of free speech and to accept all the consequences of this choice....We believe that our chance to build up here eventually a great institution among the colleges of the world will be far better if we stand for truth and freedom, than if we silently consent to yield our minds to any sort of intellectual bondage." Bassett was not dismissed. During Theodore Roosevelt's visit to Trinity campus in October, 1905, he praised the school's stand on behalf of academic freedom. *The South Atlantic Quarterly* is still being published; in December, 1977, it celebrated its 75th year.

Photograph courtesy of Duke University Archives

Epworth Inn, on Trinity's campus, was built in 1892 as a gift of Washington Duke. Heated with warm air and lighted with electricity, it contained 75 dormitory rooms, a parlor, the college chapel, a reading room, and a dining hall seating 250.

Photograph courtesy of Duke University Archives

The Mary Duke Building on the Trinity College campus was the first women's dormitory, built as a memorial to the daughter of Washington Duke, Mary Duke Lyon. It contained 11 dormitory rooms, a parlor, a dining room, bathrooms, and linen rooms.

Photograph courtesy of Duke University Archives

Twenty to thirty teams of mules, together with wagons, workers, and construction equipment, are seen at the circa 1925 groundbreaking for one of the buildings at Trinity College. The edifice on the right with white stone corners and dome was the old library. The building with the two pyramid-like towers is Alspaugh Hall. Among those present at the groundbreaking were R. L. Flowers, Sybil Flowers, Horace Trumbauer, Frank Clyde Brown, and Nello Teer.

Photograph courtesy of Duke University Archives

January 2, 1926: a view of Trinity College, which was in the process of becoming Duke University. The foundation of the Carr Building occupies most of the picture. On the right is Craven Memorial Auditorium; behind it is Alspaugh and the school library, all of which were removed shortly after the time of this photograph.

Photograph courtesy of Duke University Archives

Trinity College faculty, 1904.

Photograph courtesy of Duke University Archives

William Preston Few (1867-1940) was president of Trinity College from 1910 to 1924 and of Duke University from 1924 to 1940. After receiving his Ph.D. in modern languages from Harvard, he joined the Trinity College faculty in 1896 and became dean in 1902. His good relations with the Duke family were significant in laying the groundwork for what evolved into the Duke Endowment and Duke University. He is shown here, right, with his wife; Doris Duke stands at left.

Photograph courtesy of Duke University Archives

Diggings for the construction of Duke University's East Campus. Dr. Frank Clyde Brown, a member of the English Department of the college, served as overseer through much of the campus' construction. Brown stands upon the steam shovel, wearing a straw hat. The two women have not been identified.

Three Trinity College buildings, Craven Memorial Hall, Alspaugh, and the school library, were removed to make way for the development of Duke University. These buildings were given by Benjamin Duke to Kittrell College in Kittrell, North Carolina.

Photograph courtesy of Duke University Manuscript Department

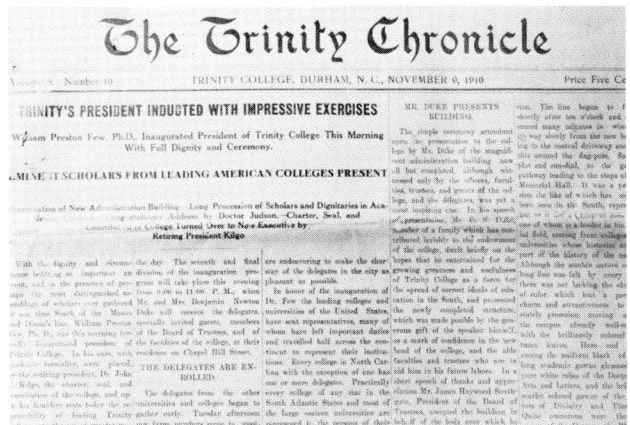

Newspaper courtesy of Duke University Archives

Horace Trumbauer drew up several plans for the construction of Duke University. Since the Dukes were fond of water, this and other plans showed provisions for fountains, man-made lakes, and various other water displays. The fountain in the right foreground and the lake near it (site of the Sarah P. Duke Gardens) were not built since building funds dwindled as costs rose.

Drawing by Horace Trumbauer, courtesy of Duke University Archives

Doris Duke, daughter of James B. Duke, lays the cornerstone for Duke University's new West Campus on June 5, 1928. Dr. Frederick Shannon, speaker for the occasion, stands on the left, and George G. Allen, chairman of the board of trustees of the Duke Endowment, is on the right.

Photograph courtesy of Duke University Archives

The East Campus of Duke University as photographed in the late 1930's. When James B. Duke's plans to change Trinity College into a major university became known, the land surrounding Trinity and Watts Hospital quickly became much more expensive. Land at a distance to the west of Trinity was purchased for the expansion of the school; therefore, Duke University is divided into East and West Campuses.

When John T. Still signed the building permit on January 14, 1928, for construction of East Campus, it was the largest single building permit in Southern history at that time. The cost was seven million dollars. No permit was necessary for the construction of West Campus, since it was then not a part of the city.

This aerial photograph shows the East Campus as it was redesigned and rebuilt between 1925 and 1928 in Georgian style by architect Horace Trumbauer.

Photograph courtesy of Duke University Archives

Duke University's West Campus under construction, May 3, 1930. The library and the medical school are prominent. The School of Medicine opened October 1, 1930, and was dedicated April 20, 1931. The building materials were brought to the site by rail.

Photograph courtesy of Duke University Archives

The choice of stone for the Collegiate Gothic buildings of Duke University was of great interest to James B. Duke. Samples of stone from nearby Hillsborough and several quarries in the North were inspected. In late March, 1925, Duke and the trustees of the endowment overwhelmingly designated the Hillsborough stone for use. Shown here is early excavation of the Hillsborough quarry.

Photograph courtesy of Duke University Archives

Despite all the generous gifts from Washington Duke, Benjamin N. Duke, and James B. Duke to Trinity, Duke, and other institutions, this is the only picture of any one of them in academic apparel. Benjamin Duke is at the far left. The occasion is the inauguration of William Preston Few as president of Trinity College.

Photograph courtesy of Duke University Archives

Installation of the carillon at Duke University Chapel in May, 1930. The 50-bell carillon was made by John Taylor and Company of Loughton, England, bell founders since 1360. It was a gift of George G. Allen and William R. Perkins, chairman and vice president of the board of trustees of the Duke Endowment. The carillon has a range of over four octaves, with the diameters of the bells ranging from eight inches to six feet, nine inches. The bells vary in weight from ten pounds to eleven thousand two hundred pounds. The first carillon recital was played by Anton Brees.

Photograph courtesy of Duke University Archives

Dedication of the Sarah P. Duke Gardens on Friday afternoon, April 21, 1939. Left to right are: Dr. R. L. Flowers, Dr. Fred M. Hanes, Norfleet Webb, Mrs. Ellen Shipman (architect), Mrs. Mary Duke Biddle, President William P. Few, and Colonel John F. Bruton.

Photograph courtesy of Duke University Archives

The Sarah P. Duke Memorial Gardens, located on 50 acres of Duke University's West Campus, presently receive more than 100,000 yearly visitors. Given by Mary Duke Biddle in honor of her mother, they were opened to the public in 1938. These photographs were made in the early 1930's, when the gardens were known as the Iris Gardens.

Photograph courtesy of North Carolina Collection, Wilson Library, University of North Carolina, Chapel Hill

Photograph courtesy of Duke University Manuscript Department

Inside the Duke University Chapel. The Chapel itself has undergone few changes since its completion. In 1971 a large light that was wrapped in a canvas covering was left burning all night. The canvas caught fire and dropped onto the first pews, and during the night, the first eleven pews were burned. They have since been replaced by chairs, and many consider this to be a more flexible arrangement. A new million-dollar Flentrop organ was dedicated in 1976.

Photograph courtesy of North Carolina Collection, Wilson Library, University of North Carolina, Chapel Hill

The Rose Bowl Game of January 1, 1942, at Duke Stadium was the only Rose Bowl that was not held in Pasadena, California. Just weeks before the game, the Japanese bombed Pearl Harbor. The U.S. Army decided that it might well prove dangerous to the national interest if a crowd such as the annual classic would attract gathered upon the west coast. Duke, which was to play Oregon State, invited that team to come to Durham, and the Rose Bowl was held at Duke Stadium. On a rainy New Year's Day, Duke was defeated, 20-16.

The stadium has been the site of numerous athletic events, including several international track meets. Duke Stadium was dedicated October 5, 1929. The first football game in the stadium was played against a powerful Pittsburgh team. The Duke team was coached by Jim DeHart. Despite the coffin corner kicking of Eric Tipton, the Blue Devils were beaten badly.

In 1967 the stadium was renamed to honor Wallace Wade, a football coach and athletic director appointed in April, 1930. In 16 seasons of coaching at Duke, his football teams won six conference championships. At age 85, he still keeps an active interest in Duke athletics.

Photograph courtesy of Duke University Archives

Mike Gminski displays his dominance of the inside game during the Big Four Tournament in Charlotte on December 3, 1977: Duke beat Wake Forest 97-84. On March 4, 1978, Duke beat this same Wake Forest team 85-77 for the Atlantic Coast Conference Tournament Championship to qualify for the National Collegiate Athletic Association playoffs. Other players are Kenny Dennard, Frank Johnson, Larry Harrison, Leroy McDonald, Eugene Banks and Rod Griffin.

Photograph by Bill Setliff, courtesy of Duke University Athletic Association

In March, 1978, a young Duke basketball team captured the hearts of Durham residents and students alike by placing second in the NCAA (National Collegiate Athletic Association) basketball finals in St. Louis, Missouri.

The 1977-78 Blue Devil team, finishing with a final 27-7 record, has a Cinderella story. The previous year they had placed last in the regular season of the Atlantic Coast Conference and in 1977-78 the starting five consisted of two freshmen (Eugene Banks and Kenny Dennard), two sophomores (Mike Gminski and John Harrell), and one junior (Jim Spanarkel). By the end of the season, the team had jelled. They won the Atlantic Coast Conference Tournament by beating Wake Forest 85-77 in the finals. Rhode Island and Pennsylvania were the next to fall in the NCAA Eastern Regionals; Villanova was trounced 90-72 for the regional championship. Notre Dame fell victim 90-86 in the semi-finals. Duke then lost to top-ranked Kentucky 94-88 in the championship game.

The transformation from a team relatively unknown outside the region to second place in the national tournament came about through the intensive drive and determination of the players, superb coaching by Bill Foster (elected as co-coach of the year by the National Association of Basketball Coaches), and the enthusiastic support of the Blue Devil fans. Upon arriving home, the team was greeted with a pair of signs that said it all: "No. 2 on the charts—No. 1 in our hearts."

Duke University Varsity Basketball Team, 1977-78. From left, kneeling: Coach Bill Foster, Captain Jim Spanarkel; seated: Kenny Dennard, Bob Bender, John Harrell, Steve Gray, Rob Hardy, Bruce Bell, Jim Suddath; standing: Assistant Coach Lou Goetz, Assistant Coach Ray Jones, Manager Kevin Hannon, Manager Mary Kay Bass, Harold Morrison, Cameron Hall, Mike Gminski, Scott Goetsch, Eugene Banks, Trainer Max Crowder, Manager Debbie Ridley, and Assistant Coach Bob Wenzel.

Photograph courtesy of Duke University Athletic Association

North Carolina Central University

Prior to 1910, the Reverend James Shepard had been a member of the International Sunday School Association, and within this organization it was his duty to represent the Sourthern blacks. Through his work with the Association, Shepard determined that members of the black clergy were almost always poorly trained.

In the year 1910, with aid from Brodie Duke and the Durham Merchants Association, Shepard started the National Religious Training School and Chautauqua with the aim of educating the black clergy. Shepard soon discovered that those who came to his school were usually deficient in knowledge of general academic subjects. In 1916, the school's original aim of training people for the ministry was forsaken, and Shepard's institution became the National Training School, which satisfied the purpose of providing a general academic education for its black students.

By 1925 the school, then called North Carolina College, became the first state-supported liberal arts college for black people in the United States. In 1969, the name of the school was changed to North Carolina Central University, and in 1972, together with 15 other senior institutions, became a part of The University of North Carolina.

Photograph courtesy of State Division of Archives and History

Dining Hall, North Carolina College.

Postcard courtesy of Duke University Manuscript Department

An aerial view of the North Carolina College of Durham as photographed shortly after the close of World War II. James E. Shepard, the school's founder and president, comported himself with great dignity, yet he felt compelled to deliver weekly pep talks to the school teams to spur them on to victory. In his gruff tones he would conclude his speeches: "Remember you are Eagles. And the Eagle is no common barnyard fowl."

Photograph courtesy of North Carolina Collection, Wilson Library, University of North Carolina, Chapel Hill

Dr. Leroy T. Walker was the head coach for the men's track and field events for the 1976 United States Olympic team. This deserved honor resulted from his remarkable record in developing some of our country's most outstanding sprinters and hurdlers at North Carolina Central University. His collaborations with Al Buehler at Duke have been instrumental in bringing premier talent to several international track meets and in promoting Durham as the track capital of the world.

Photograph courtesy of Durham Chamber of Commerce

The Clyde Hoey Administration Building (1929), the oldest building on the campus, honors a North Carolina governor and a United States Senator. Most of the institution's original structures were destroyed by fire.

Postcard courtesy of Duke University Manuscript Department

Durham College

Photograph courtesy of Durham College

Muhammed Ali addresses a Durham College audience on December 6, 1977, at dedication ceremonies for a new multi-purpose athletic facility named in his honor. Among the guests on the platform, from left, are: Stephanie Calloway, president of Student Government Association; Dr. Lucinda McCauley Harris, founder of Durham College; Vivian Edmonds, editor and publisher of the *Carolina Times*, a weekly Durham newspaper; The Reverend Lorenzo Lynch, pastor, White Rock Baptist Church; James W. Hill, president of Durham College; Ralph Hunt, city councilman; and Barbara Amos, instructor at Durham College.

Durham Technical Institute

Durham Technical Institute, located at 1637 Lawson, offers both day and night classes, on and off campus. The curriculum now contains 25 major programs with 17 programs leading to an Associate in Applied Science degree. The student body is composed of over 2,500 students.

The origin of the Institute can be traced back to June, 1948, when a program of practical nursing was established under the Vocational and Adult Education Department of the Durham City Schools. Other programs, including mechanical drafting, architectural drafting, and electronics technology, were developed in the following years. Courses were conducted mostly at night in classrooms and laboratories at Durham and Hillside High Schools.

By 1957, the North Carolina General Assembly authorized an appropriation to establish a limited

Photograph by Joel A. Kostyu

The school was organized on November 16, 1947, by Dr. Harris, with the purpose of training youth for business-oriented careers. Dr. Harris had resigned her job in a local high school and was so enthusiastic about her goal that she carried her typewriter from door to door while soliciting funds for the school. Initial enrollment was five male students. The school has expanded to its present location at 3128 Fayetteville Street. After several name changes, it took the name Durham College in 1971, the same year that the institution was nationally accredited as a junior college of business.

number of schools to be known as Industrial Education Centers to provide facilities for training or improving skills of workers in a variety of trades and for offering other educational opportunities. Durham's adult education program was already in full swing.

In June, 1958, the residents of Durham County made $500,000 available for the purchase of a site and an initial building. The Durham Industrial Education Center opened its doors on September 5, 1961, with 34 full-time students. On March 30, 1965, the board of trustees authorized the name of the school to be changed to Durham Technical Institute. It is a charter member of the North Carolina Department of Community Colleges and is a member of the Southern Association of Colleges and Schools.

Photograph courtesy of Durham Technical Institute

PEOPLE: THE LIFEBLOOD OF DURHAM

A city may have everything going for it—industry, attractive neighborhoods, excellent educational opportunities, fine stores, and many other attributes—but in the long run, people shape a city. Durham has been fortunate; it has a heritage which reveals a people who continue to look ahead.

Durham's institutions of higher education have attracted many notables to the city. These "guests," along with the devoted residents and solid, working citizens, have created an enviable civic pride. The human drama that is Durham pulses on!

J. W. Cheek operated a store on the southwest corner of Main and Mangum Streets in about 1858. He became Magistrate of Police in 1869 and later Durham's first mayor.

Photograph courtesy of Wyatt T. Dixon

Malbourne Angier, an early merchant of Durham, was born in 1820. In the 1850's he operated a store at the northwest corner of Main and Mangum Streets. Once a member of the North Carolina General Assembly and chairman of the board of county commissioners, he was one of Durham's first mayors and a magistrate for 50 years.

Photograph courtesy of Wyatt T. Dixon

About 1910, Hugh Mangum posed the family for a picture. Hugh, kneeling at the lower right, is squeezing a bulb to trip the camera. Pressley J. Mangum, a Durham postmaster, is seated. The family lived in the now restored McCown-Mangum house near the West Point mill at the Eno River Park near Durham.

Photograph courtesy of Margaret Nygard

The William J. Mangum family posed in front of their home, where General Sherman had stayed during the conferences at Bennett Place.

Photograph courtesy of Wyatt T. Dixon

The governing board of Durham in 1895 consisted of Mayor Isaac N. Link and aldermen Leo D. Heartt, H. J. Bass, A. D. Markham, J. W. Carlton, James W. Walker, W. H. Proctor, and C. A. Jordan. The city had 6,000 residents at the time.

Photograph from Handbook of Durham, *published by the Educator Company, 1895*

Grave number one at Maplewood Cemetery has an ironic story behind it. The city purchased the cemetery site in 1872 over the objections of Lewis Alston. He contended that a baseball field was needed more than a publicly owned cemetery. In a post-election celebration across from the Blackwell factory, a Civil War cannon belonging to W. T. Blackwell was fired. After a number of shots, the hot gun exploded and Alston was killed. He occupies grave number one in the cemetery.

Photograph courtesy of Wyatt T. Dixon

Photograph courtesy of Duke University Archives

Dignitaries have often stopped in Durham. However, on October 19, 1905, a historical event took place when Theodore Roosevelt, twenty-fifth President of the United States, was welcomed by Durham citizens to the Trinity College campus. Twelve thousand people, including the faculty and students, heard President Roosevelt speak on academic freedom, leadership, and service.

He said, in part: "I have been across this Union from the Pacific to the Atlantic, from the Canada line to the Gulf, and the one thing that has impressed me most wherever I have been in addressing the various audiences has been their fundamental likeness—the fact that wherever you go in this country, the average American is a pretty decent fellow, and the only thing necessary to make him get on well with any other average American is to know him. And now, men who wore the gray and men who wore the blue, and their sons, stand alike as citizens of this one country, alike in their loyalty to our common flag, and knowing but one rivalry— the rivalry as to which can do the most for their country and that flag."

Photograph courtesy of Duke University Archives

A 1936 graduate of Duke, Les Brown went on to become famous with his Band of Renown.

Photograph courtesy of Duke University Archives

In 1912 President Roosevelt made a train stop in Durham. The writer of this card tells how the nephews of Laura Holton had to run down the track a half-mile to catch up with the train.

Postcard courtesy of Stephen Massengill

The 78th "Lightning" Division marching down Main Street drew crowds of people. The division was formally activated August 15, 1942. They played a major role in battles on the European front. Edwin P. Parker was commander of the division.

Photograph courtesy of Wyatt T. Dixon

W. C. Davison, dean of the Duke School of Medicine, at left, with Doris Duke Cromwell, and W. H. Wannamaker, vice chancellor of Duke, attends the christening of two Liberty ships, the *James B. Duke* and *W. P. Few*, in Brunswick, Georgia, June, 1944.

Photograph courtesy of Duke University Archives

Al DeRogatis looks mean in this 1948 photograph at Duke Stadium. No wonder, with no face mask! An All-American lineman, he went on to play in the National Football League. He is now a vice president for the Prudential Life Insurance Company.

Photograph courtesy of Duke University Archives

Ralph Bunche, winner of the 1950 Nobel Peace Prize, is shown speaking at Duke. He was the first black to head a division of the United States State Department. Later, as a top official of the United Nations, he helped settle many international disputes.

Photograph courtesy of Duke University Archives

Governor William Bradley Umstead, North Carolina's only governor from Durham County, was buried on November 9, 1954, in the Mount Tabor Methodist Church graveyard after a state funeral at Trinity United Methodist Church. Umstead was the first governor to die in office since 1874.

William Umstead grew up on a farm. As a congressman (1933-1939) he supported such measures as soil conservation, crop control programs, and rural electrification. He was also instrumental in securing during the Depression an emergency loan of over $500,000 from the Reconstruction Finance Corporation for the North Carolina Mutual, assisting that company through those traumatic years. Later he served as a United States Senator. Two days after his inauguration to the statehouse, he had a severe heart attack and for almost two years governed from his bed at Watts Hospital or from the governor's mansion in Raleigh.

Photograph courtesy of State Division of Archives and History

Dave Sime, who received his bachelor's and medical degrees at Duke, was a world-class sprinter. Originally coming to Duke on a baseball scholarship, he was so fast that the track coach noticed him. At one time he held a world record. While in medical school, he won the silver medal in the 100-meter dash in the 1960 Rome Olympics. The winner and he established the Olympic record at that distance at 10.2 seconds in a close finish. Dr. Sime is an ophthamologist in Florida.

Photograph courtesy of Duke University Archives

Durham celebrated its centennial on April 26, 1953. Members of the executive committee of the Durham Historical and Centennial Commission are shown. From left, seated: J. Frank Jarman, pageant; Frank A. Pierson, secretary; M. Arnold Briggs, chairman; Floyd Fletcher, co-chairman; A. M. Harris, hospitality. Standing: John L. Moorhead, publicity; O. Gordon Perry, spectacle tickets; Leo Spaeth, representative of the John B. Rogers Producing Company which staged the pageant; Marcus Carpenter, special events; Ernest S. Booth, treasurer. One of the methods used to spark interest in the celebration was a requirement that men grow mustaches or beards. Those without a shaver's permit were thrown into "jail." John L. Moorhead was the only member of the group above who used the shaver's permit.

Photograph courtesy of Wyatt T. Dixon

Mayor Emanuel J. Evans, A. W. Kennon, Governor Luther Hodges, and Adlai Stevenson at a rally on October 21, 1960.

Photograph courtesy of Duke University Archives

Mary Duke Biddle Trent Semans, Howard Wilkinson (university chaplain), Beth Semans, Madame Karolou (lady-in-waiting to Princess Irene), Her Royal Highness Princess Irene of Greece, and Mrs. Douglas Knight (wife of Duke's president) pose in front of Duke Chapel, January 28, 1967.

Photograph courtesy of Duke University Archives

Angier Biddle Duke, Ben E. Powell, and R. Taylor Cole pose for the presentation of Ambassador Duke's papers to the Duke Library on April 28, 1968. Dr. Cole, Provost, substituted for President Douglas Knight, who was ill.

Photograph courtesy of Duke University Archives

Walter Cronkite of the CBS Evening News receives from Terry Sanford, Duke University president, an honorary degree of Doctor of Letters at 1972 commencement exercises. At left stands Otto Meier, Jr., university marshall.

Photograph courtesy of Duke University Archives

Richard M. Nixon, Pat Nixon, and daughters Julie and Tricia Nixon. Mr. Nixon graduated from Duke Law School with honors in 1937. He served as a congressman, as Vice President, and later as President of the United States.

Photograph courtesy of Duke University Archives

Carr grave in Maplewood Cemetery was commissioned at a cost of $40,000. The six major figures are carved of Italian marble sculpted in Italy. The poem is on a bronze tablet on the back of an angel. A portion reads:

I closely held within my arms
    A jewel rare:
Never had one so rich and pure
    Engaged my care.
'Twas my own, my precious jewel—
    God gave it me.

Photograph by Frank A. Kostyu

Gerald Ford visited Durham when he was a congressman from Michigan and again as President of the United States. He visited the campus of North Carolina Central University in November, 1975. Theodore Roosevelt was the only other President to visit Durham while in office.

Photograph courtesy of Duke University Archives

The Dukes

Many prominent persons have contributed to the growth of Durham; a number of them appear in the pages of this book. But the most famous family is the Duke family, whose members brought a new dimension of American enterprise not only to Durham but also to the nation. It is said that when Washington Duke returned from the Civil War in 1865, he walked from New Bern to his Durham home, now a state and national historic landmark, with cash assets totaling one silver dollar, given to him by a Union soldier in exchange for a five dollar Confederate note. His other possessions included a 300-acre farm, a wagon, two mules, and some tobacco.

By hand, he flailed, sifted, graded, and packed the tobacco and then peddled it by wagon. He used the brand name "Pro Bono Publico." Money being scarce, he would often barter his tobacco for other commodities.

Out of these humble beginnings grew an industry and an empire. The Dukes pioneered a world-wide mass market in cigarettes. But their interests were rooted also in textiles, hydroelectric power, banking, and education. Few can point an accusing finger and admonish the Dukes for not being generous with their wealth. Duke University stands as one monument to their generosity and philanthropy.

Washington Duke was born December 20, 1820, one of ten children of Taylor Duke, who lived in what is now the Bahama section of Durham County. Duke was twice married. Mary C. Clinton, his first wife, died November 18, 1847; she was the mother of Sydney T., who died at 14, and Brodie L. Duke. Washington Duke married Artelia Roney on December 9, 1852; she was the mother of Mary, Benjamin Newton, and James Buchanan Duke. She died August 20, 1858, of typhoid fever.

On May 8, 1905, Washington Duke died. Durham's businesses and schools closed. His pew at the Main Street Methodist Church was draped in black. People from all walks of life followed the funeral procession to Maplewood Cemetery. In the April 16, 1900, edition of the *Durham Recorder*, it had been stated that Duke's aim was to help make the world better for having lived in it.

Photograph courtesy of the Duke Homestead Tobacco Museum

Brodie Leonidas Duke (1846-1919) was very much involved in the development of Durham. He had interests in tobacco, textiles, railways, real estate, and mercantile establishments. Brodie Duke had more extensive real estate holdings than any other family member. At the same time that his father, Washington Duke, and his two younger brothers began the manufacture of tobacco at their homestead, Brodie Duke independently grew the leaf on his own farm.

In 1869, Brodie Duke moved into the town of Durham to expand his business. For a time, his factory was in the same building as that of his father and two younger brothers; a partition running through the building was all that separated the two enterprises. He did not enter into formal partnership with his father and brothers until 1878.

Photograph courtesy of Duke University Manuscript Department

Mary Elizabeth Duke Lyon (1853-1893) was actively engaged in the development of the Duke tobacco industry. Daughter of Washington and Artelia Roney Duke, she helped in packing tobacco in drawstring bags and in keeping house. Later she married Robert E. Lyon, a dealer in leaf tobacco, and had five children. She died at age 39 after a prolonged illness.

Photograph courtesy of Duke University Manuscript Department and the Duke Homestead Tobacco Museum

James Buchanan Duke (1856-1925) was the major driving force in developing the W. Duke, Sons and Company into the giant American Tobacco Company. His vigor and acumen for business opportunities also led to the establishment of the Duke Power Company. His generous endowment to what became known as Duke University has brought this institution into world prominence.

Photograph courtesy of Duke University Manuscript Department and the Duke Homestead Tobacco Museum

Benjamin Newton Duke (1855-1929) often seemed to stay out of the limelight, yet he was keenly involved in the Dukes' business affairs. He became the family's chief agent for philanthropy as he helped establish the financial and educational foundations of Trinity College. In addition, he concerned himself with the development of what is now North Carolina Central University and other institutions in the Southeast, including hospitals and orphanages.

Photograph courtesy of Duke University Manuscript Department and the Duke Homestead Tobacco Museum

Sarah Pearson Angier married Benjamin N. Duke in 1877.

Photograph courtesy of Duke University Manuscript Department

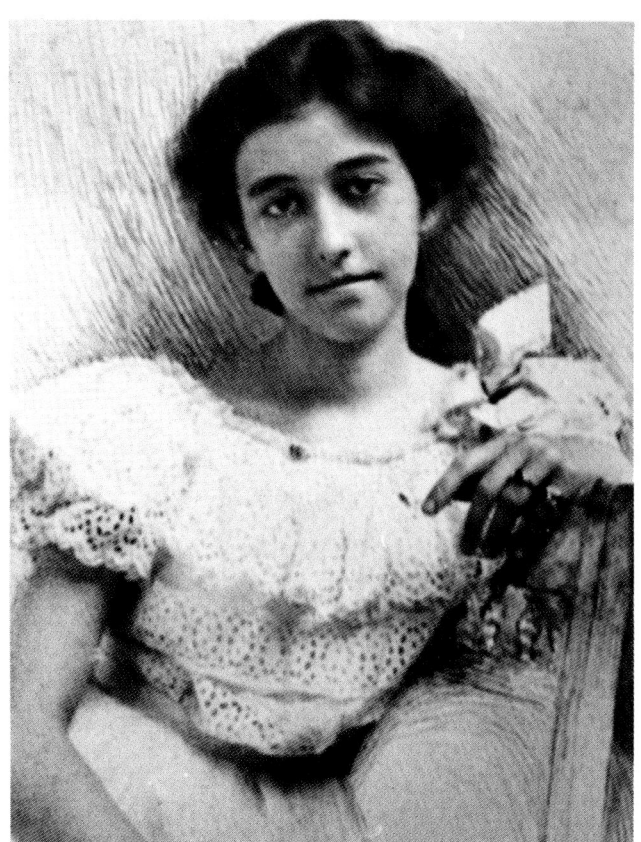

James Buchanan Duke at age 16 or 17. He was named after a Democratic President since his father, Washington Duke, was a Democrat up to the time of the Civil War.

Photograph courtesy of Duke University Archives

James B. Duke, often called Buck, is on the left, while Benjamin N. Duke is on the right. Washington Duke is purported to have said that there were only three things he couldn't understand: the sun rising in the east and setting in the west, the Holy Ghost, and his son Buck.

Photograph courtesy of State Division of Archives and History

Nanaline Holt Duke, born in Macon, Georgia, in 1871, was the second wife of James B. Duke and the mother of his only child, Doris. James B. Duke at age 57 took great pride in becoming a father. Mrs. Duke died on April 12, 1962.

Photograph courtesy of Duke University Archives

Washington Duke as he appeared late in life. About ten years before his death, Washington Duke was described by Robert Watson Winston, a young Durham lawyer: "The stout old gentleman, with shaven upper lip and short-cropped beard on his ample chin and face, wearing a stiff hat, about such as Oliver Cromwell would have worn, and dressed in a plain, untailored dark suit, would slowly enter my office and quietly sit and tell of his scant young days and of the folly of the old secession leaders, who had brought on the Civil War."

Photograph courtesy of Duke University Archives

The funeral procession for James B. Duke on October 13, 1925, was a sad time for all of Durham. Duke had become ill in July of the same year with what was later diagnosed as pernicious anemia. Duke's condition worsened with time, and he finally succumbed on October 10, 1925, in his Fifth Avenue mansion in New York. After a private service, Duke's body was carried by train back to Durham, where services were conducted at Duke Memorial United Methodist Church.

Photograph courtesy of Wyatt T. Dixon

James B. Duke was buried in the family mausoleum at Maplewood Cemetery.

Photograph courtesy of Wyatt T. Dixon

Today the remains of Washington Duke, Benjamin Newton Duke, and James Buchanan Duke lie in the Memorial Chapel to the left of the chancel in the Duke University Chapel.

Photograph courtesy of Duke University Archives

Fairview, at the southeast corner of Main and Duke Streets, was built by Washington Duke after he retired in the mid-1890's. Note that his residence stands near the second Duke Tobacco Works. The white building between home and factory was a hothouse. This picture was taken about 1895 looking northeast from Peabody Street, which ran along the north side of the North Carolina Railroad tracks.

Photograph courtesy of Duke University Manuscript Department

DURHAM'S HOUSES

Profound philosophical, political, economic, and social changes marked the late nineteenth century. Durham citizens, many among the richest in the state, chose varying architectural styles for the houses and commercial buildings they erected, including: Queen Anne, Italianate, Second Empire, Romanesque, and Second Renaissance styles. Nearer the turn of the century, the Neo-classical Revival style, featuring columned porticos and large spacious rooms, began to dominate the elegant, tree-lined streetscapes.

Pictured here are architectural examples built for the early residents of Durham, and the reader can easily observe the variety of designs. Some of these lovely homes are gone; many have been preserved.

Julian S. Carr's house at Dillard Street, called Waverly Manor, is shown here. In the late 1880's, it was carefully dismantled, removed, and re-erected on the south side of Peabody Street near Dillard to make way for Somerset Villa.

Photograph courtesy of Duke University Manuscript Department

Excavation was begun on July 31, 1887, and the cornerstone to Somerset Villa was laid September 29, 1888. Among the contents of the cornerstone were: copies of *The Tobacco Plant*, September 27 and 28, 1888; Hiram Paul's *History of Durham*; Confederate money of all denominations; charter of the town of Durham, adopted January 19, 1886; Bull Durham smoking tobacco, vintage 1888; the first five dollar bill issued by the First National Bank, signed by J. S. Carr, president, and Leo D. Heartt, cashier; and a copy of the Holy Bible. The house was demolished in the 1920's.

Photograph courtesy of Durham Chamber of Commerce

This 1883 photograph shows Brodie L. Duke's home on the land between Morgan, Minerva, Gregson, and Duke Streets, the present site of Durham High School and Carr Junior High School. Duke is standing on the ground floor of the house, next to his wife, Martha V. McMannen Duke. Students sometimes visited the pond behind the house to collect water lily stems for botany class. The house was razed in 1919.

Photograph courtesy of Duke University Manuscript Department

This radiator with a built-in plate warmer was among the unusual features of Four Acres.

Photograph courtesy of Duke University Manuscript Department

Four Acres, the home of Benjamin Duke, as photographed shortly after construction was completed in 1911 at a cost of $136,000. The house stood on the southeast corner of Duke and Chapel Hill Streets; it was torn down in about 1960. It is the present site of the North Carolina Mutual Life Insurance Company.

Photograph courtesy of Duke University Manuscript Department

Inside Four acres.

Photograph courtesy of Duke University Manuscript Department

The home of William T. Blackwell, located at the corner of Chapel Hill and Duke Streets, in a photo taken about 1905. The site is now occupied by the Duke Memorial United Methodist Church. Blackwell went into banking after his success in the tobacco business. He once said that he used to take a long time getting home from work. However, after his Bank of Durham failed in November, 1888, his trip was much quicker; no one stopped to talk to him on the way home.

Photograph courtesy of Duke University Manuscript Department

John Merrick, founder of North Carolina Mutual Life Insurance Company, is shown on the balcony of his spacious Victorian home at 506 Fayetteville Street, circa 1910. The house is no longer standing.

Photograph courtesy of North Carolina Mutual Life Insurance Company

This photograph shows Benjamin Duke's home before he built Four Acres on the same site. A goat cart such as the one shown here was a wonderful source of enjoyment for the young children of well-to-do families of Durham.

Photograph courtesy of Duke University Manuscript Department

The John Sprunt Hill house recently has been placed in the National Register of Historic Places. The building was designed by Kendall and Taylor of Boston in 1911 for Hill (1869-1961), a lawyer, banker, businessman, politician, and social leader of extensive statewide influence. Today the house is the headquarters of the Junior League of Durham. According to John Sprunt Hill's will, the building may not be demolished.

Photograph by Frank A. Kostyu

A 1977 view of the home known as the "President's House" at 504 Watts Avenue. A shingle-style home with turreted bay and conical roof, it was built in 1891 for John F. Crowell, president of Trinity College.

Photograph by Frank A. Kostyu

The home of E. J. Parrish stood at the corner of Dillard and East Main Streets. When he went to Japan in 1898 to represent the American Tobacco Company, Parrish sold the house to R. H. Wright. The home of C. B. Green was next door, at left in this photo. Note the stepping stones across Main Street. They came in quite handy on rainy days when the unpaved streets became seas of mud.

Photograph courtesy of Duke University Manuscript Department

The Markham house on Cleveland Street was to the north of and adjacent to the First Baptist Church. It was torn down in 1972.

Photograph by Jim Thornton, courtesy of Wyatt T. Dixon

Harwood Hall, the residence of George W. Watts, was on Proctor near Duke Street. It has been razed.

Photograph courtesy of North Carolina Collection, Wilson Library, University of North Carolina, Chapel Hill

The Pegram house has known three locations. Built in 1891, it was located on Faculty Row on what is now Duke's East Campus. In 1915 it was moved, using logs and teams of horses, to 308 Buchanan. This photograph was taken in 1977 just prior to its being moved to a vacant lot at 1019 Minerva to make way for a parking lot. Through the efforts of the Historic Preservation Society of Durham, the house was preserved for its architectural and historical significance.

Photograph by Frank A. Kostyu

The Benjamin Franklin Kronheimer house, Rosevilla, at 1015 Minerva was built in 1930 in the Second Renaissance Revival style. Kronheimer was an early Durham dry goods merchant.

Photograph by Frank A. Kostyu

The W. H. Wannamaker House at 1019 Trinity is noted for its shingle-covered crenelated tower. It was built in 1891 and originally stood on Faculty Row, where it was the home of Dr. Wannamaker, dean of Trinity College and vice-chancellor of Duke University.

Photograph by Frank A. Kostyu

The James E. Stagg House at 618 Morehead Avenue is a chateau-style yellow stone mansion, one of the few remaining in North Carolina. It was designed by Charles C. Hook of Charlotte and was built in 1911 by N. Underwood. The interior woodwork is executed mostly in walnut and mahogany. Today it is divided into apartment units.

Photograph by Frank A. Kostyu

HOUSES OF WORSHIP

As Durham's commercial activities took root, churches were established and became a part of the social and cultural life of the community. Churches formed the focal points for many activities on Sunday as well as during the week. News regarding the community was eagerly discussed after services.

It is interesting to note that in 1892, when the Erwin Cotton Mill was opened, the company employed 375 hands, all of whom resided on the premises in conveniently arranged houses belonging to the company. For the benefit of these employees, "a nice church building" was erected in close proximity to the mill. The Pearl Cotton Mill also provided a church building on their premises.

The early pioneers of Durham, such as Duke, Carr, Watts, and others, not only were benefactors of the early churches, but also active participants in the life of the church. It is said of G. W. Watts, a business colleague of the Duke family, that for more than 20 years he walked faithfully across town every Sunday afternoon to attend Sunday school.

On the ashes of the old church, a new Trinity Church of Gothic Revival style was built under the guidance of the Reverend W. W. Peele. The architectural firm of Cram and Fergerson of Boston designed the building. The first worship service was held on September 20, 1925. The vitality of Durham's oldest congregation continues in this building.

Postcard courtesy of Duke University Manuscript Department

Willis Haynes, a Methodist circuit rider, brought Methodism to the Durham area in 1832. Durham's first Methodist Church was a plain, wooden structure named Orange Grove Methodist Church, located on Roxboro Road. In 1860 the congregation moved to Durham. One and one-half acres were purchased from William Green, and the church was built by William Mangum at a cost of $650. Trustees of this church were William J. Duke, Washington Duke, Archibald Nichols, D. M. Cheek, James Cheek, Z. I. Lyon, and John Barbee. In 1866 the Orange Grove Methodist Church changed its name to the Durham Methodist Church.

In 1880 the cornerstone was laid for a new, brick, Victorian-style building on Church Street, shown here. The Durham Methodist congregation changed its name to Trinity Methodist Church in 1886. As Durham grew, so did Trinity Church. When the structure was destroyed by a spectacular fire early Sunday morning, January 21, 1923, there was fear that the magnificent tall spire would fall and injure many people. However, it crashed into the burning ruins below.

Photograph courtesy of Duke University

The railroad provided the Baptist congregation with four acres of land on what is now Cleveland Street in exchange for their property and building near the railroad as partial payment. This second building was completed in 1854.

Drawing courtesy of First Baptist Church

The history of the present First Baptist Church dates back to August 12, 1845, when services were held under the name of Rose of Sharon Baptist Church in the Piney Grove School House, one mile south of what is now West Durham. In 1850 the first church building of the congregation, shown here, was located at what is now the 100 block of Pettigrew Street. The North Carolina Railroad, although a vital instrument in establishing Durham, was a problem to the worshipers in the new church; the noisy locomotives interrupted worship and frightened the horses of the parishioners.

Drawing courtesy of First Baptist Church

In 1878 the name of the Baptist Church was changed to Durham Baptist Church, and the original name was taken by a congregation north of town. In 1878 a portion of the property was sold, except for what is the present site of the church, and the present name of First Baptist Church was adopted. Property on Mangum Street was bought and a brick structure built which served the church from 1895 to 1927. The expansion of the church and its programs necessitated additional facilities. Under a committee headed by Willis J. Brogden, the present structure (except for the south wing) was begun in May, 1926, and completed in September, 1927. Reuben Harrison Hunt of Chattanooga, Tennessee, was the architect.

Drawing courtesy of First Baptist Church

The cornerstone of the present White Rock Baptist Church.

Photograph by Frank A. Kostyu

White Rock Baptist Church, 3400 Fayetteville Street, dedicated its new church building Sunday, October 23, 1977. The congregation was organized in 1866 by Margaret Faucette and later moved to the 600 block of Fayetteville Street. This property was purchased by Urban Renewal in 1967, and the congregation worshiped and served in interim quarters until it occupied its next building in 1971. W. E. Jenkins of Greensboro was the architect and J. M. Dixon, Inc., was the contractor.

The church is located on more than six acres of land, three acres of which are to be developed into a park-playground area with facilities for baseball, football, basketball, and other community sports. A devastating ice storm in January, 1978, bent the tower structure.

Photograph by Frank A. Kostyu

This stereoscopic photograph shows the new First Presbyterian Church, built in 1890 on the same site, at Main and Roxboro.

Photograph courtesy of Blackwell Brogden

The Presbyterians organized as a congregation on December 31, 1871, but Dr. Richard Blacknall and his family, who came to the town in 1860, have been credited as the first of their denomination to reside in Durham. For a time, the handful of members worshiped in the Baptist and Methodist churches. In 1874 impetus was generated to erect a building of their own, and in 1875 a plain, wooden structure was erected on Main near Roxboro with the Reverend H. T. Darnell as resident pastor. In 1890 a brick structure was built on the original site.

This photograph reveals some conditions quite common in those early days. The dirt roadway had ditches on either side to carry off the rain water. The residential properties were usually surrounded by picket fences, although well-to-do families sometimes had fences of wrought iron. The street lamp was little more than a kerosene lamp on a pole.

Photograph courtesy of Wyatt T. Dixon

In 1916 the present First Presbyterian Church was built to accommodate the expanding congregation and church programs. This photograph was taken in 1946.

Photograph courtesy of Wootten-Moulton Studios

St. Joseph's African Methodist Episcopal Church. The A.M.E. Church has its roots in the Free African Society, an organization founded in 1787 by Richard Allen and Absolom Jones, two black Philadelphia ministers, for the purpose of a self-help beneficial brotherhood. The A.M.E. Church, rooted in these tenets, became the first autonomous black church in America. St. Joseph's cornerstone was laid in 1891. The church was built with a metal ceiling and painted glass windows; the window in this photograph represents Washington Duke. On a visit to Durham, Booker T. Washington once said, "In all my traveling, I have never seen a finer Negro Church than St. Joseph's."

Slated for demolition in 1976, the church was saved by the St. Joseph's Historic Foundation, an outgrowth of the Historic Preservation Society of Durham.

*Photograph by Randall Paige,
courtesy of State Division of Archives and History*

The Temple Baptist Church was organized on January 29, 1888. In the early 1880's, the pastor of the Durham Baptist Church, the Reverend C. C. Durham, led in the establishment of afternoon Sunday schools in various sections of the growing city of Durham. One of these gatherings was located on South Duke Street in a building owned by James W. Blackwell. Within two years, a building was erected on West Chapel Hill Street with W. T. Blackwell and W. G. Vickers providing the property and materials for construction. The first pastor was C. C. Newton, who was paid an annual salary of $700. Within the first ten years of its existence, the church had six ministers.

The name of the church was changed to Blackwell Baptist Church in 1888, then in 1890 to The Second Baptist Church. At some time between 1917 and 1919, the name was changed to Temple Baptist Church, and so it remains to this day.

In 1957 a new $425,000 sanctuary was built on Arnette Avenue and West Chapel Hill Street. In 1961 the building committee was reactivated in order to construct new educational facilities.

Photograph courtesy of Wyatt T. Dixon

Duke Memorial United Methodist Church, prior to the 1931 additions. The rapid growth of the Durham community gave rise to the need for more than one Methodist church. From the original Trinity Methodist Church grew the West End Church (later to become Duke Memorial United Methodist Church) and East End Church (later to become Carr Methodist Church). Early meetings of the West End Church were held at the W. Duke, Sons, and Company tobacco factory; the East End congregation met at the Durham Cotton Manufacturing Company.

On October 10, 1886, the West End Church, also known as the Bethany Sunday School, moved into a permanent home on the southeast corner of Main and Gregson Streets, on land donated by Brodie L. Duke. April 24, 1887, saw the Main Street Methodist Church formally dedicated.

The rapid growth of population and the coming of Trinity College to Durham in 1892 led to an expanding congregation. The Main Street Church was sold to the Christian Church in November, 1906, for $6,500. The property on the corner of Duke and Chapel Hill Streets, formerly belonging to William T. Blackwell, was chosen as the site for a new church. The Dillon Supply Company purchased the old Main Street property; the former sanctuary was torn down to make room for a parking lot. The portion of the church that had been used for Sunday school was converted into an office building.

On June 7, 1914, the new church was dedicated, with Bishop John C. Kilgo, former president of Trinity College, presiding. The name of the church became Duke Memorial Methodist Episcopal Church, South, generally acknowledged as a memorial to Washington Duke and the Duke family for their financial and personal support.

Postcard courtesy of Duke University Manuscript Department

Around 1881-82, some 300 members of the Jewish faith settled in Durham, mainly working in the W. T. Blackwell and the W. Duke, Sons, and Company tobacco factories. At that time cigarettes were made by hand, and upon the advent of the Bonsack cigarette machine, many Jews returned north. During the 1890's, a congregation worshiped on the third floor of what was known as Dr. Johnson's Building at 102½ East Main Street. On November 20, 1902, the congregation incorporated under the name of Durham Hebrew Congregation, its purpose being for religious, literary, and charitable practices, and sought to establish and maintain a Jewish cemetery in Durham.

Around the turn of the century, the congregation acquired a building on Liberty Street formerly occupied by the Christian Church. In 1918, the house of worship was sold to the city so that Queen Street could be extended. The synagogue pictured here, at the corner of Queen and Holloway Streets, was completed in 1921. The board of directors recommended on April 15, 1921, that the name of the congregation be changed to Beth-El, Incorporated. On February 17, 1957, the ground was broken for the new Beth-El Synagogue and Center at Watts and Markham Streets.

Photograph courtesy of Wyatt T. Dixon

The Duke Chapel was the last major building constructed on the West Campus as designed by architect Horace Trumbauer of Philadelphia. The cornerstone was laid October 22, 1930. The Chapel has become the focal point of West Campus, symbolic of the importance with which the Duke family regarded religion and university life. Such famous theologians as Reinhold Niebuhr, Paul Tillich, Albert Outler, Martin Niemoller, and evangelist Billy Graham have delivered sermons in the Duke Chapel.

This picture was taken in the 1930's, when the building was under construction; the pews and altar had not yet been installed. Seventy-seven stained glass windows depict Old and New Testament figures and stories, with some 900 figures represented in the various biblical scenes.

Photograph courtesy of Duke University Manuscript Department

The first building for the Immaculate Conception Catholic Church was dedicated in 1906, built on property on West Chapel Hill Street donated by William Thomas O'Brien. The roots of the congregation can be traced back to the 1870's, when Father Mark Gross and Father James B. White would come from Raleigh to hold mass in the home of Mrs. James Lawrence, the first Catholic to reside in Durham. Her husband worked for William T. Blackwell and is credited with the invention of the Lawrence cigarette packing machine, which was used for many years.

The development of the Bonsack machine for making cigarettes had a pivotal effect on the Catholic Church in Durham. William Thomas O'Brien came to Durham in 1881 to run the Bonsack machine in the Duke tobacco factory. O'Brien perfected the machine that became instrumental in the development of the cigarette industry and the Duke fortune. The O'Brien home on Wilkerson Avenue was the center for worship services until the construction of the church. O'Brien died just two weeks after its dedication.

As missionary pastor, Father Michael Irwin served the congregation from 1901 to 1907. William Francis O'Brien, who served the parish for more than 40 years, was appointed the first resident Roman Catholic pastor of Durham. At the time, only about 110 Catholics resided in the town. A new church, located on the site of the original building, was dedicated in 1957.

Photograph courtesy of Polly McGurk

Although the Duke Chapel's 210-foot tower is patterned after one at Canterbury Cathedral in England, the Gothic, cruciform chapel itself had no particular mold. This 1977 photograph shows the statue of James B. Duke, which stands before Duke Chapel. It is interesting to note that James Duke, who made his fortune manufacturing cigarettes and cigarette tobacco, is holding his ever-present cigar. It was said he did not enjoy smoking cigarettes. For occasional celebrations, Duke University students "dress" Mr. Duke in campus finery.

Photograph by Frank A. Kostyu

St. Philip's Protestant Episcopal Church had its beginnings in 1878 when services, held in Duke's Hall on Main Street, were conducted by Joseph Blount Cheshire, later Bishop of North Carolina. He led the small band of Christians until 1880, when a congregation was formally organized. There were 11 original members. The church building erected in 1880 on the present site is portrayed here on a stereoscopic photograph.

Photograph courtesy of Blackwell Brogden

The building in use today was designed by Ralph Adams Cram of Boston, architect of such notable edifices as the Cathedral of St. John the Divine in New York and buildings at Princeton University. The brass appointments of the 1880 church are still used, the memorial windows were added about 30 years ago, and the altar window memorializes Sidney Stuart Bost, the rector from 1898-1936.

Photograph by Frank A. Kostyu

COMMUNICATION & ENTERTAINMENT

Cultural development was not neglected during the rapid growth of early Durham. In October, 1896, the Up-to-Date Club was established to hear literary criticism and to debate current events; one of their early topics was "electricity." The Up-To-Date Club is considered one of the oldest women's clubs in the state. Other turn-of-the-century organizations included the Lyceum, St. Cecilia Society, Tourist Club, Social Science Club, Commonwealth Club, Canterbury Club, and Duke's Campus Club.

Country clubs, tennis and gun clubs, college sports, and the Piedmont League—a professional minor league baseball team—provided recreation; numerous small parks are still located throughout the city. As a sign of our times, a shopping center now stands on part of what was once Lakewood Park, where early Durhamites could swim, roller skate, hear the band play, and picnic with family and friends.

During the 1880's and 1890's, public halls first became available for music recitals, political gatherings, and traveling shows. Stokes Hall was the most prominent early one. In 1904, the elegant Academy of Music was erected, largely with Duke family support.

Communication via the printed and the spoken word is always an important aspect of the life and growth of a community. Durham's experience in bringing the news and entertainment to its citizens is no exception. A number of small papers specializing in subjects of local interest appeared through the early history of Durham; however, four main newspapers emerged as purveyors of information: *The Tobacco Plant, The Durham Recorder, The Durham Sun*, and the *Durham Morning Herald*.

Radio has also played a vital role in Durham's history. Late in February, 1934, Durham's first radio station, WDNC, came to the community. A group of interested citizens made a deal with Harris Newman to purchase WRAM in Wilmington, North Carolina, and to move the station to Durham, with the approval of the Federal Radio Commission. Within one hour after leaving the air in Wilmington, the station's transmitting equipment and studio effects were taken down, loaded on a truck, and shipped to Durham, where the studios, offices, control room, and transmitter were located on the top floor of the Washington Duke Hotel. Two towers were erected on the hotel roof to carry the single-strand antenna wire. The manager of the new station was E. W. Carr, who had managed the Wilmington station.

Popular Norfley Whitted was director of black affairs for the station and, according to WDNC, the first black disc jockey in the South and among the first in the nation; he had four shows on the air.

Two television stations serve Durham: WRDU, channel 28, is the NBC affiliate, and WTVD, channel 11, is the CBS affiliate. One of WTVD's notable former broadcasters is David Hartman, now host of "Good Morning America."

The cultural life of Durham continues to be vital. The Durham Arts Council, previously known as United Arts (1954) and Allied Arts (1961), supports many local cultural groups by providing facilities, administrative and financial assistance, and publicity from its headquarters in the Foushee house on Proctor near Vickers Avenue. It supports such diverse groups as the Council for Creative Arts in the Public Schools, the Art Guild, Dance Associates, the Civic Choral Society, the Chamber Music Guild, the Durham Savoyards theater group, the Durham Theatre Guild, and the Photographic Arts Society. It is also involved in programs for senior citizens as well as neighborhood and city arts programs.

Street fairs and craft shows are often sponsored by private organizations, by the city, or by the Durham Arts Council, which is the second oldest community arts program in North Carolina. The Durham Symphony, the Pocket Theatre, New Performing Dance Company, the Ciompi Quartet, North Carolina Chamber Players, the Summer Theatre at Duke, the Duke Players, National Opera Company Summer Season, the American Musical Theatre Center, and the newly arrived American Dance Festival, round out a rich and varied cultural environment which has given Durham a new name: The City of the Arts in the State of the Arts.

Many towns had a local band. The Durham Brass Band dates back to about 1884. The members of the band shown here, about 1900, were Charley Murphy, George Lougee, Jack Thomas, Edgar Cheek, John Seeman, W. R. Murray, Jack Wilborn, Joe H. King, and "Sonny" Cheek.

Photograph courtesy of Wyatt T. Dixon

Durham Orchestra. This photograph, taken about 1904 or 1905, hangs in the lobby of the Seeman Printery on Chapel Hill Boulevard. In the front row, from left, are Ernest Seeman, J. H. King, Kimbro Jones, Dan Albright, and Mr. Stockard. In the back row are George E. Lougee, W. E. Seeman, Ernest Markham, and Pleas Pickard.

Photograph courtesy of Seeman Printery

The joy of a circus parade! On May 28, 1895, a parade was photographed heading west to Lyon Park, located across Morehead Avenue from Maplewood Cemetery. The size of the crowd standing along the street reflects the small population of Durham, about 6,000, at this time. The streets were mostly unpaved and the walks were of slate. The awnings on the storefronts protected shoppers from the sun and rain.

Lyon Park was used for baseball and football. The first night game in the area was played there—a softball game between a touring Indian team and a Durham team. The Indians won!

Photograph courtesy of Wyatt T. Dixon

This early twentieth century photograph shows a recital at the Southern Conservatory of Music.

Photograph courtesy of Wyatt T. Dixon

Lakewood Park was the primary amusement center of Durham from about 1905 to 1926. Richard Wright, who owned the franchise for the transportation company, the electric light company, and a telephone company, built the park. There were a swimming pool, roller skating rink, a roller coaster, and a merry-go-round. This photograph shows one of the open-sided electric trolley cars that stopped at Lakewood Park.

Photograph courtesy of Wyatt T. Dixon

Frances Moss Jarman of WDNC radio interviews Perry Como in the late 1950's on one of his frequent visits to Durham. Mrs. Jarman was at one time known as North Carolina's first lady of radio; she did three shows a day for five days a week. In addition, she did spot news before it was widely practiced.

Photograph courtesy of WDNC Radio, Whitely and Scott photographers

The Grand Theater, "The Home of Good Pictures," was a popular motion picture house in 1912. From what we see in the photograph, the Grand offered a choice of films: Tyrone Power in *Aristocracy, The Circus Man* with Theodore Roberts, and *Joey and His Trombone*. On the day the photograph was taken, two comedies and three dramas were offered for the price of 5¢ and 10¢.

Photograph courtesy of Wyatt T. Dixon

This page from *The Tobacco Plant* displays what is sometimes known as the Southgate map, showing Durham and the surrounding communities. Of particular interest are drawings of various city scenes and industries, demonstrating the vitality and progress of the young community.

The Tobacco Plant was established in January, 1872, by Caleb B. Green, brother of John Ruffin Green of tobacco fame. It was a weekly periodical at the time, serving the county. In September, 1886, the paper was sold to Julian S. Carr, and in June, 1888, became a daily, *The Daily Tobacco Plant*, with J. B. Whitaker named editor in September of that year.

Newspaper courtesy of State Division of Archives and History

The 1924 Durham baseball club.

Photograph courtesy of Duke University Manuscript Department

The *Durham Sun* saluted WDNC Radio in February, 1949, on the occasion of an increase in power. The station first went on the air in April, 1934, with a program sponsored by Liggett and Myers for Chesterfield. CBS dedicated a quarter-hour program welcoming WDNC as the forty-first station to join the network.

Early in 1936, the stock of the Durham Radio Corporation was acquired by the Durham Herald Company, publishers of *The Herald* and *The Sun*. In 1939, new studios were constructed and the location was changed to 138 East Chapel Hill Street on the second floor of the B. C. Woodall Company.

Featured in this newspaper salute to WDNC are (1) William Keighley; (2) Abe Burrows and Milton Delugg; (3) Todd Russell of "Strike It Rich"; (4) Win Elliot of "County Fair"; (5) Bob Crosby and Janet Waldo (Corliss Archer); (6) The Andrews Sisters; (7) Julie Conway, Armstrong's Quaker Girl on "Theater of Today."

Newspaper courtesy of Ed Higgins

In 1892, *The Daily Tobacco Plant* was purchased by Edward A. Oldham and assumed the name *Durham Globe*. Oldham retained ownership only three months, and the paper returned to the control of Julian S. Carr. After a rather turbulent history, during which it changed owners several times, in July, 1895, the paper was sold to R. H. Cowan, who reorganized it from a daily to a weekly once more.

This action left J. H. King, J. T. Christian, W. W. Thompson, and Z. P. Council out of work. Thereupon they bought from Washington Duke an

old press of the by-then defunct *Durham Recorder* and started *The Globe Herald*. After a short time, the name of the paper was changed to *The Morning Herald*. King and Thompson stayed with *The Morning Herald* until the latter sold his share to E. T. Rollins, Sr.

Posing here in front of the Market Street offices in 1905 are, left to right: R. H. Cowan, J. H. King, and E. T. Rollins, Sr. This was the first company-owned building of *The Morning Herald*; it was built on a lot purchased from John Sprunt Hill.

Photograph courtesy of Wyatt T. Dixon

Does anyone have a wrench? Not too many friends are coming to the rescue. Bicycling was a popular pastime at the turn of the century. Barring slipped chains, a flat tire, or a bent wheel, bicycling in the country was a Sunday afternoon fun sport. Note that this particular photograph depicts an all-male outing—and, of course, everyone wore a hat or a cap.

Photograph courtesy of Mr. and Mrs. George C. Pyne, Jr.

Vince Simonetti, conductor of the Durham Symphony Orchestra, directs the 60-person orchestra before an audience of 300 at Durham's Five Points, July 22, 1977.

Photograph by Jim Thornton, Durham Morning Herald

The *Durham Morning Herald* spared no pains when it had a movie made for the city. *Durham's Hero* was a comedy, and all the characters were played by Durham citizens. Alfred Griggs was the hero. The first showing of the movie was on February 23, 1925, at the Paris Theater. The film was well received; the house was packed for a week. The wreck scene was staged at the corner of Main and Corcoran Streets. Many of the bystanders are on the steps of the old Post Office.

Photograph courtesy of Duke University Manuscript Department

FASHION

Significant changes took place in fashions at the turn of the century as both men and women began to wear clothing plainer in style and color. Simple fabrics, including muslin, cotton, and wool, replaced sumptuous brocade, velvet, and silk, and replaced the beads, buttons, fringes, and lace ruffles which decorated nineteenth century fashions. By 1910 the long tubular hobble skirt had become popular, and a distinctive mode in early fashions was the tailored suit, consisting of a long jacket with an ankle-length skirt.

The wealthy women of Durham kept up with the fashions of New York and Paris. The men, not so fashion-conscious, nevertheless kept up with the styles. Fashion changed, too, for firemen, soldiers, and others.

Two members of the Durham Light Infantry, organized in 1878.

Photograph courtesy of Wyatt T. Dixon

Will Mangum shows the fireman's uniform he proudly wore in the early days of the development of the fire department. The "dress-up" outfit was worn especially at parades.

Photograph courtesy of Wyatt T. Dixon

This postcard from early 1912 shows a miss sporting the style of the times.

Postcard courtesy of Stephen Massengill

Lila Bingham Markham married William James Brogden in January, 1917. She is shown in her wedding clothes.

Photograph courtesy of Blackwell Brogden

Mamie Dowd claimed that she was the first girl in Durham to own a bicycle. She posed for this shot in a photographer's studio.

Photograph courtesy of Mr. and Mrs. George C. Pyne, Jr.

Mamie Dowd Walker, shown in 1904 in the dress she wore for her marriage to Fielding L. Walker, was a Durham native and Judge of Juvenile Court.

Photograph courtesy of Mr. and Mrs. George C. Pyne, Jr.

Two gowns worn by Sarah Duke, photographed in the early 1950's when they were on display at Four Acres. On the left is her wedding dress; on the right is her silver anniversary gown.

Photograph courtesy of Duke University Manuscript Department

The war years were difficult times, and luxuries were at a premium. When nylon hosiery was put on sale at the Woolworth store in downtown Durham, the place was mobbed by men and women hoping to get a pair. Nylon, a new synthetic fiber, was valuable in the war effort, especially in the production of parachutes.

Photograph courtesy of Wyatt T. Dixon

Candid photographs were not the thing in the early 1900's, but these ladies do appear to be enjoying their lollipops.

Photograph courtesy of Mr. and Mrs. George C. Pyne, Jr.

Durham Fire Department's racing team is shown here on the day of competition in the early 1900's on Cleveland Street. These annual races took place between fire departments of some of the larger North Carolina cities. The Durham team felt they had two of the fastest horses in the state. The team would race down the street for a distance, the firemen jumping off at a hydrant. The first team to start pumping the water was declared the winner. Bleachers were for the fans as well as for competing drill team members.

Photograph courtesy of Wyatt T. Dixon

The hook and ladder wagon of the fire department at the turn of the century.

Photograph courtesy of Wyatt T. Dixon

The Main Street Fire House, Fire House #2, was erected in 1906; it was located on the north side of West Main and Duke Streets, near the site of the Liggett-Myers Company offices.

Photograph courtesy of Durham Chamber of Commerce

Dennis C. Christian was the last fire chief of the horse-drawn era. Fire Chief from February 1, 1909 to June 1, 1921, he is shown seated in the chief's buggy in front of Fire Station #1 at Mangum and Holloway Streets. The building was torn down and a new one was built to accommodate motorized vehicles. The second building still stands, its exterior practically unchanged.

Photograph courtesy of Wyatt T. Dixon

ALL AROUND THE TOWN

Many stories emerge about the beginnings of a city. One of these relates to the location of Main Street. Legend has it that Isaac N. Link, an early surveyor of Durham County, got into a saloon argument on the laying-out of Durham streets with another customer. A fight developed. The antagonists agreed that wherever their heads hit the ground, that would be the boundary of Main Street. And so it goes.

The streets of Durham have changed in more ways than the camera has recorded. Street names evolved, too: In 1883, Clay Street became Parrish Street, and was extended in 1888 from Church to Roxboro Streets when Captain E. J. Parrish granted consent for a right-of-way through his property; in 1887, South Rail Road became Pettigrew Street, Raleigh Street became Ramseur Street, Depot Street became Corcoran Street, and Durham Avenue became Peabody Street.

Durham marked November 3, 1977, with a parade of bands, horses, old-time cars, and color guards to celebrate the addition of the downtown commercial district to the National Register of Historic Places, a movement led by the Historic Preservation Society. A certificate was presented to Durham's Mayor Wade Cavin by Sara Hodgkins, secretary of the North Carolina Department of Cultural Resources.

The designation of downtown Durham as a historic district was the first in North Carolina for an exclusively commercial area. A number of the buildings of note reflect beaux-arts, classicism, and art deco styles of commercial architecture with elegant exterior detail.

Viewing these street scenes will take the reader back in time.

Julian Carr stands before Confederate veterans gathered to celebrate a May 10 Confederate Memorial Day at the turn of the century.

The elegant 70-room Hotel Carrolina, developed by Julian S. Carr, was one of the finest hotels in the South. The wood structure featured guest rooms with frescoes painted by Italian artists and paneled public rooms containing expensive tapestries decorated in various period motifs: Louis XV, Louis XVI, Empire, Old English, and Victorian.

The Carrolina was on the site of Bartlett Durham's home, Pandora's Box, and subsequently the Hotel Clairborne. Built in 1891, the Carrolina burned in a dramatic fire in May of 1907. A branch of the Durham Hosiery Mills then occupied the spot for many years. A parking lot is now located there.

Photograph courtesy of Duke University Manuscript Department

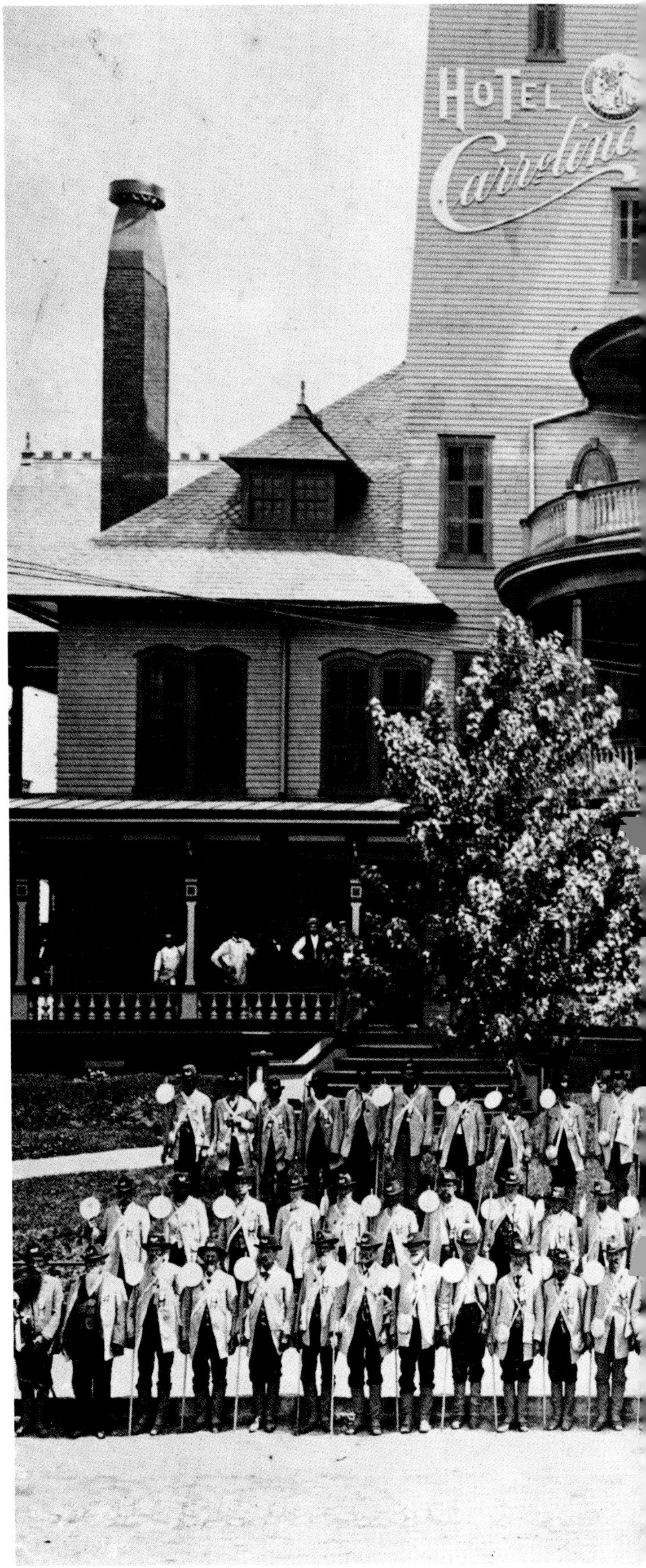

A postcard draws attention to Durham and its excellent accommodations.

Postcard courtesy of Stephen Massengill

POST CARD.

THE ADDRESS TO BE WRITTEN ON THIS SIDE

HOTEL CARROLINA, one of the most costly, attractive hotels south of Washington, is regarded as the "Half-way House" to the winter tourist in his journeyings to and from the South. New, modern and elegant, with generous piazzas, a sun parlor, and all appointments of a first-class house, it is popular at all seasons of the year.

Raphael Tuck & Sons' "Raphotype" [Reg'd] Postcard No 5088, "DURHAM, N. C."

ART PUBLISHERS TO THEIR MAJESTIES THE KING & QUEEN.

Miss Josie Parrish,
956 Haile St.
Staunton,

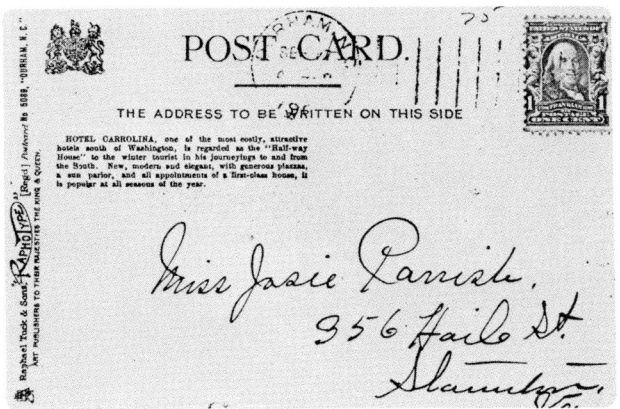

The Biltmore Hotel in its prime, when it was featured on postcards as a Durham attraction. The hotel was built for use by blacks visiting Durham. Several shops occupied the ground floor.

Postcard courtesy of Stephen Massengill

Biltmore Hotel, January, 1977, reflects the change in the integrated South. Separate black hotels are no longer needed, so the old Biltmore will be demolished. It is reported that it will be torn down brick by brick and that these bricks will be cleaned by unemployed youth and resold.

Photograph by Frank A. Kostyu

The Durham Hotel stood at the corner of East Main and Church Streets. The Hotel McArthur was just north of it. In this photo, policemen converse with a man in uniform, and a firehose extends from the hydrant into the building. We can see by a poster that a Tim McCoy movie, *Riders of Black Mountain*, was playing at the nearby Criterion Theatre.

Photograph courtesy of Wyatt T. Dixon

On the northwest corner of Main and Roxboro Streets was the Malbourne Hotel, built in 1913. Next to it is the Rialto Theatre. At the time this photo was taken, the upper floor of the theatre building was leased to the hotel to provide for its growing needs. The Western Union telegraph office is shown on the left. With the construction of the Washington Duke Hotel, the Malbourne suffered from a lack of patronage and was torn down in the fall of 1966.

Photograph courtesy of Wyatt T. Dixon

Another view of the Malbourne Hotel made circa 1913 during its prime.

Postcard courtesy of Stephen Massengill

The Beverly Apartments at Watts Street and Main Street were owned by George Watts and were Durham's first apartments built solely as an apartment complex. The revenue from the apartments went to support Watts Hospital.

Postcard courtesy of Stephen Massengill

A Durham landmark, the Washington Duke Hotel, is shown under construction in 1924.

Photograph courtesy of Wyatt T. Dixon

This photo shows the Washington Duke Hotel after its completion. It opened the night of October 21, 1925, with a five-dollar-a-plate banquet.

Photograph courtesy of Durham Chamber of Commerce

The first Durham County Courthouse, at the southeast corner of Church and Main Streets, is shown here at the turn of the century. To the right of the building is the spot where the only two hangings in the city's history took place, in the early 1900's. A white man was executed for the murder of his wife, and a black man for committing first degree burglary.

Photograph courtesy of Wyatt T. Dixon

This is the way the Washington Duke Hotel appeared in the early 1970's. It had been known under other names—the Jack Tar Hotel and the Durham Hotel—but for many it carried the remembrance of Washington Duke and a nostalgic past. On a December morning in 1975, the Durham landmark was imploded.

Photograph courtesy of Wyatt T. Dixon

The Franklin Court Apartments at Main Street east of Dillard Street were known for their excellent accommodations. They were torn down in the 1960's and replaced by Oldham Towers.

Postcard courtesy of Stephen Massengill

Durham County Courthouse on East Main Street was constructed of Indiana limestone of neo-classical revival style and designed by the Milburn and Heister Company of Washington D.C. It was completed in 1916. The new judicial building is to be occupied in 1978.

Photograph by Frank A. Kostyu

Main Street normally had much activity. In this early 1900's picture, looking east from Church Street, is Herndon's Drug Store on the left in the Inter-State Telephone Building. On the right is the first county courthouse. The heavy telephone cables made many such street scenes rather unsightly. Trolley tracks ran down the middle of Main Street.

Photograph courtesy of Wyatt T. Dixon

McPherson Hospital, located at 1110 West Main Street, was founded on March 23, 1926, by Samuel Dace McPherson, who administered it until his death in 1953. He was succeeded by Samuel D. McPherson, Jr., his son. The site of the first corneal transplant in North Carolina, McPherson Hospital provides training for eye, ear, nose, and throat residents and residents in opthalmology. A new addition to the right of the original building shown here was necessary to accommodate expanding needs.

Photograph by Joel A. Kostyu

The Durham County General Hospital is located on a 50-plus acre site bounded by Roxboro Road, Olympic Avenue and Stadium Drive, Duke Street, and Crutchfield Street. The precast stone T-shaped building contains 484,620 square feet and 487 beds.

On November 5, 1968, Durham County voters passed a bond issue for 20 million dollars and Hill-Burton funds supplied an additional 1.5 million dollars. Ground breaking ceremonies, held on June 19, 1972, were followed by initial excavations on July 7, 1972. The Durham County Hospital Corporation was joined by Watts Hospital on June 22, 1971, and by Lincoln Hospital on February 26, 1973.

Durham County General officially opened on October 10, 1976, with emergency rooms, the intensive care unit, operating rooms, and labor and delivery rooms in functional readiness. From 7 a.m. to 11 a.m., 123 patients were transported the 2½ miles from Watts Hospital to the new hospital. The move took 12 ambulances, 26 ambulance drivers, 12 nurses and 12 corpsmen, many from Fort Bragg and the reserve station in Durham. James Scott Blackburn, born at 8:23 a.m., has the distinction of being the first baby born at Durham County General.

An interesting anecdote, related by Richard L. Myers, assistant administrative director of Durham County General Hospital, has become attached to the opening of the new hospital. Shortly after its opening on October 10, a man arrived at the Raleigh-Durham Airport in the late evening. After renting a car, he made his way towards Durham. He got lost, but saw the hospital and headed for it. Since the hospital had just opened, not all its information signs were in place. The man parked at the emergency room entrance, walked in, stopped at the information desk, and asked for a room. When the startled clerk replied that a physician's permission was required for admittance, the traveler admitted that he thought he had stopped at the Hilton.

Photograph by Ruth Newberg

The Durham County Home, right, was the first home for indigents in the county. A water pump is at the left and some residences in the background. The buildings were erected in the 1880's but were replaced in 1924 by a single, modern building that was occupied until construction of the county hospital. This photograph was taken prior to the turn of the century and is the site of the new Durham County hospital.

Photograph courtesy of Wyatt T. Dixon

The Trust Building was Durham's first skyscraper. Erected in 1905 by John Sprunt Hill, it was then the tallest in town. It was modernized in 1933 and is now owned and occupied by Teerco. At one time the building housed the Fidelity Bank and the Home Savings Bank.

Photograph courtesy of Wyatt T. Dixon

This circa 1893 photograph shows Main Street, looking west. The Main Street Methodist Church is at the left. The tower of the Washington Duke Building at Trinity College can be seen in the distance. Gregson Street did not extend north of Main Street.

Photograph courtesy of Wyatt T. Dixon

This circa 1891 view looking west shows Washington Duke's Victorian-style home, Fairview. Main Street borders the northern portion of the property. The steeple of Main Street Methodist Church, located at the southeast corner of Main and Gregson Streets, is seen behind Fairview. An early Duke factory is at the right, and the three-story building across Main Street is the W. Duke, Sons, and Company Leaf House.

Photograph courtesy of Duke University Manuscript Department

The barns of William Mangum as they appeared in the early 1890's on Green Street, later renamed Chapel Hill Street on November 4, 1901. The property was on the north side of the street near Corcoran.

Photograph courtesy of Wyatt T. Dixon

The large elk's head hung between the second and third floors left little doubt that this was the Elks' Temple. The building, constructed in 1909 by John Sprunt Hill, now houses the Guaranty State Bank; it is located at the northwest corner of Main and Market Streets. Horses and buggies could be parked on either side of the streets—something we are not permitted to do today with our automobiles.

Photograph courtesy of Blackwell Brogden

The Academy of Music, built in 1904, served a number of different functions in its early years. The portion facing south (Parrish Street) provided offices for city officials (City Hall). The rest of the first floor was originally a meat market. The second floor was used as an auditorium. A seating capacity of more than 1,500 made this one of the largest public halls in the state. Frescoes in the concert hall were painted by Jules Korner, popularly known as Reuben Rink.

Later, after a fire gutted much of the building, the market area was redone for use as a theater. The Academy was razed in 1924 to make way for the Washington Duke Hotel. Radio comics Amos and Andy met here while performing in a minstrel show.

Postcard courtesy of Wyatt T. Dixon

Around the turn of the century, this photograph was taken of Main Street, looking west from the Trust Building. One of the buildings on the right side of the street was the town's first public library. The Hall name is still associated with Durham funeral services.

Photograph courtesy of Wyatt T. Dixon

The YMCA was organized in 1889, but ceased operation until reorganized in 1907. The large structure, built with the help of a $10,000 donation from George W. Watts and the Duke family, was located at the southwest corner of East Main and Roxboro Streets and was occupied on November 19, 1908. The YMCA building was torn down in the late 1950's, and the site is now occupied by the Durham County Office Building and Social Services. The central YMCA is now located on West Trinity Avenue.

Postcard courtesy of Stephen Massengill

The firemen on parade going west on unpaved Main Street are passing a tobacco warehouse. Firemen often staged parades to raise money for equipment or to attend racing tournaments. In the background is the tower of Stokes Hall, which served as an auditorium for various community meetings and stage performances. It stood on the northeast corner of Main and Corcoran, where the Geer Building was subsequently built. It, too, has been demolished.

Photograph courtesy of Wyatt T. Dixon

Looking south down Guess Road in Durham, 1905. This part of Guess Road has since become Buchanan Boulevard.

Photograph courtesy of Jane Edwards

From a 1910 postcard: looking west on East Main Street from near Roxboro Street. The building on the right is the first brick building erected by the First Presbyterian Church. Notice wagons clattering along on the granite and earth surface.

Photograph courtesy of Wyatt T. Dixon

Main Street, Durham, 1910.

Photograph courtesy of Duke University Manuscript Department

Street paving bricks such as these owned by Mr. and Mrs. George C. Pyne, Jr., once were a part of the Durham scene.

Photograph by Joel A. Kostyu

181

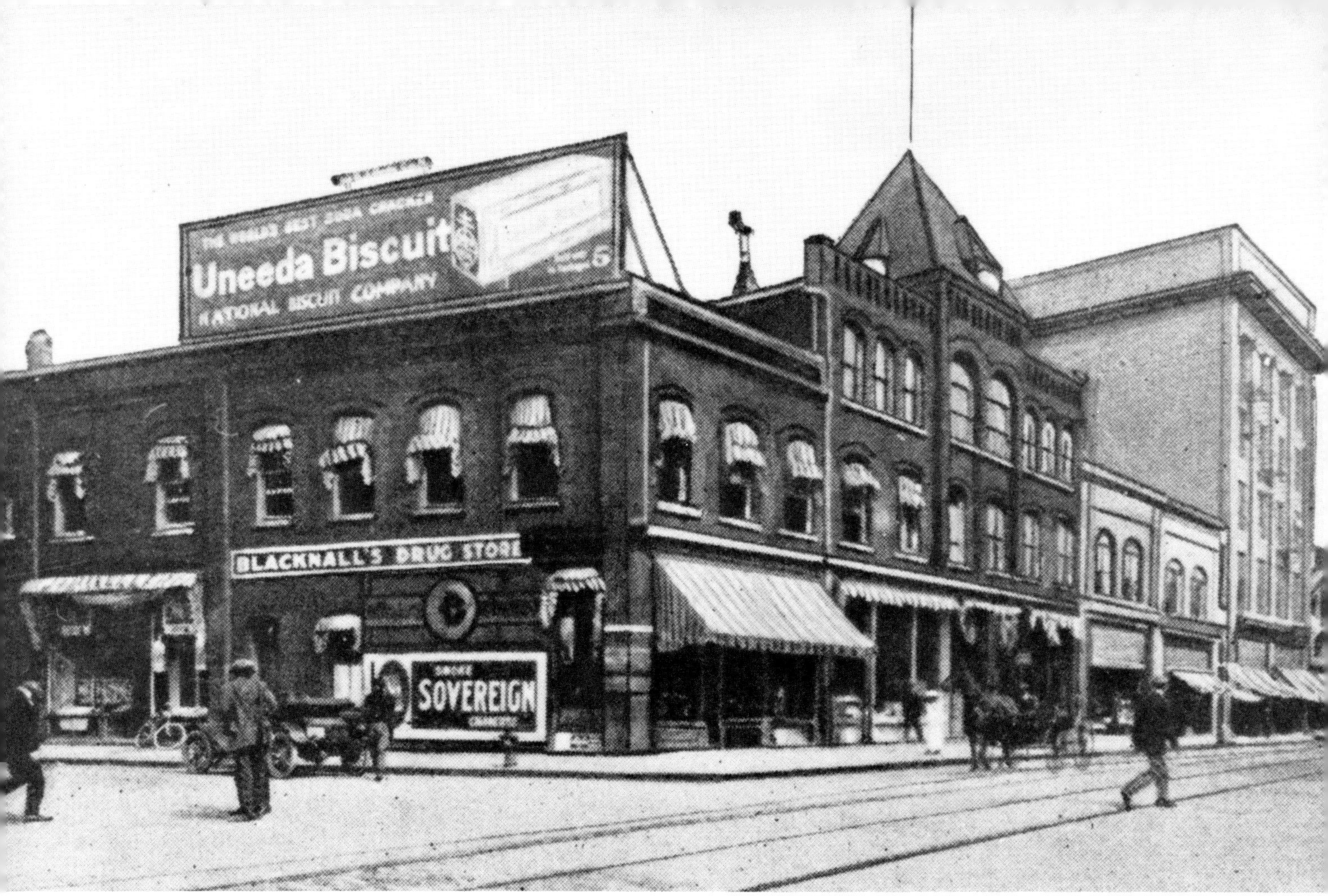
Uneeda Biscuit
NATIONAL BISCUIT COMPANY
BLACKNALL'S DRUG STORE
SOVEREIGN

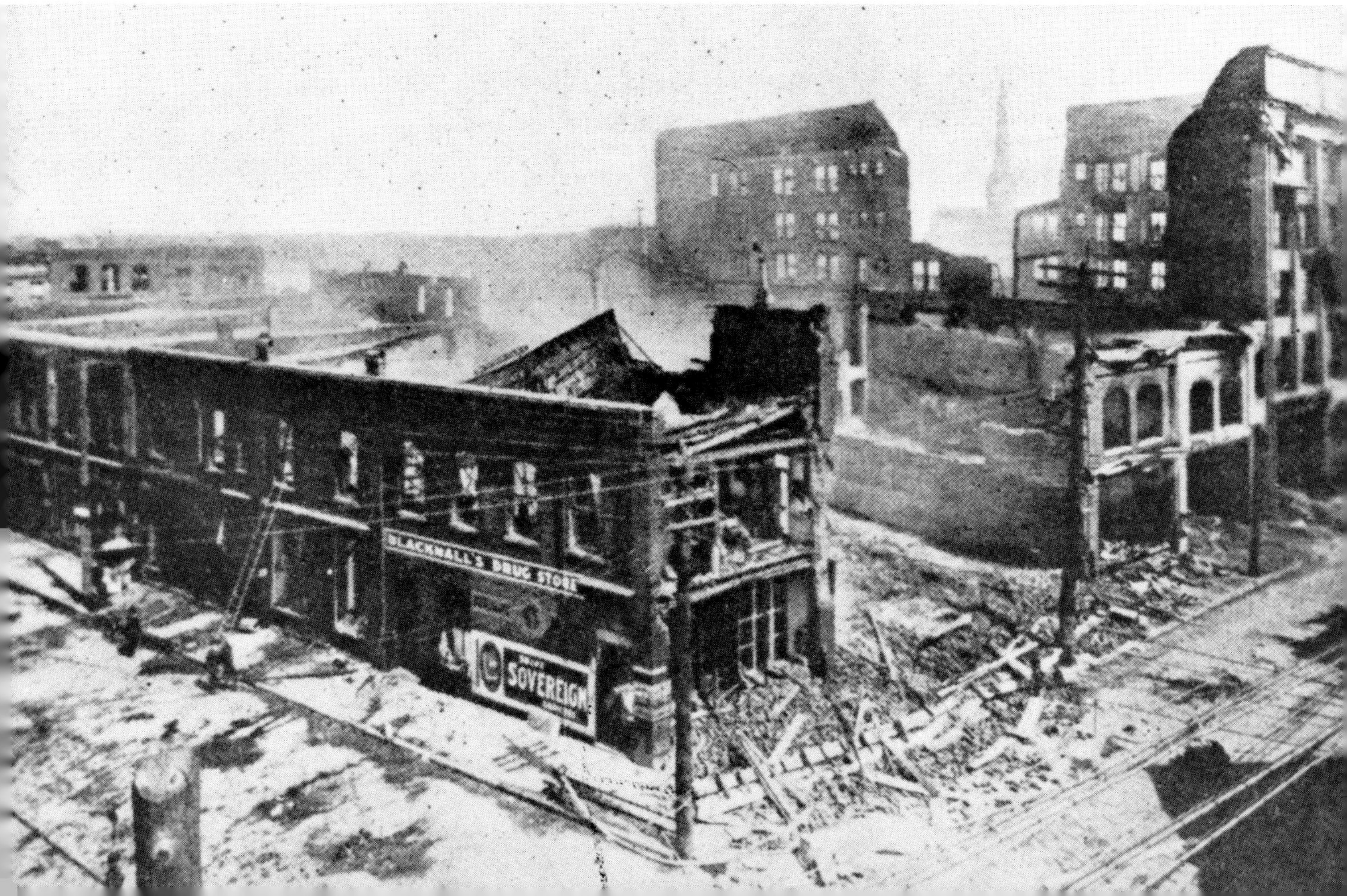
BLACKNALL'S DRUG STORE
SOVEREIGN

On the evening of March 23, 1914, the Reverend S. S. Bost, rector of St. Philips Episcopal Church, was walking downtown when he noticed fire coming from the storage warehouse of F. M. Kirby on the second floor of the Brodie Duke Building in the middle of the Main Street block (north side) between Corcoran and Mangum Streets. A disastrous fire resulted when weak water pressure left the fire department helpless to fight the blaze. The photographs were taken before and after fire ravaged one block of East Main Street.

Photograph courtesy of Duke University Manuscript Department

Carnegie Public Library at 311 East Main Street is seeing its last days as a library. First occupied in 1921, it is to be replaced by a new structure to be built nearby in 1978. Note the classical influence in the architecture.

Photograph by Frank A. Kostyu

Photograph courtesy of Duke University Manuscript Department

Durham, 1946, looking west down Parrish Street towards the 17-story Hill Building and the Washington Duke Hotel.

Central Carolina Bank and Trust Company, or CCB, which continues to occupy part of the Hill Building, traces its origins to 1903, when John Sprunt Hill organized the Durham Loan and Trust Company. Dealing primarily in real estate and insurance, its separate banking department was not established until 1915.

In 1937 the bank occupied the ground floor of the newly completed Hill Building and changed its name to the Durham Bank and Trust Company. The bank merged with the Citizens National Bank of Durham and Roxboro in 1959 and the University National Bank in Chapel Hill in 1961.

George Watts Hill, chairman of the board and son of the founder, relates how the bank got its current name: "When attorneys were instructed to draw up merger papers with the University National Bank, a UNB spokesman exclaimed, "Whoa! No loyal Carolina man can permit a 'Durham Bank' in Chapel Hill." Thus, the name Central Carolina Bank and Trust Company was born.

Photograph by Wootten-Moulton Studios

From Five Points looking west on Chapel Hill Street across the grade crossing of the North Carolina Railroad. An electric powered trolley is seen coming up Chapel Hill Street in a photo taken after 1902.

Photograph courtesy of Wyatt T. Dixon

The tracks of the trolley car system are seen in 1917, looking east on Main Street at Five Points. Durham's first public library is the first building on the left.

Photograph courtesy of Wyatt T. Dixon

West Chapel Hill Street looking east from Duke Street, 1925. The Benjamin N. Duke property is on the right. At the far end of the street, heavy equipment is being used in the construction of the railroad overpass.

Photograph courtesy of Duke University Manuscript Department

This photograph was taken about 1930 during the construction of the overpass on Chapel Hill Street. The old Benjamin Duke house is shown in the center of the picture, taken from the front yard of Thomas D. Jones. It had been moved across Chapel Hill Street to make room for Four Acres. The Herndon family house is on the right.

Photograph courtesy of Duke University Manuscript Department

Looking from Duke Street down Chapel Hill Street toward Five points. Note the Washington Duke Hotel in the background.

Construction was necessary for the creation of an overpass. The city enacted an ordinance on March 20, 1922, requiring the Southern Railway Company to abolish the grade crossing at Chapel Hill Street. Sidney C. Chambers, city attorney, sent letters to: Fairfax Harrison, president of the Southern Railway System (Washington, D.C.); S. Davies Warfield, president of the Seaboard Air Line Railway Company (Baltimore, Maryland); and A. C. Needles, president of the Norfolk and Western Railway Company (Roanoke, Virginia). Chambers asked that the required work of "carrying the street under the railroad tracks" be started within 60 days of his November 26, 1924, letter and completed in 280 days. Compliance with the ordinance had been resisted by the companies, but it was upheld by state courts and subsequently by the U. S. Supreme Court (November 17, 1923). The overpass is in use today.

Photograph courtesy of Duke University Manuscript Department

Mangum Street, Durham, January 20, 1928, looking north through one of Durham's older residential sections. Hunt Street joins Mangum Street from the right. The trolleys were still running at this time.

Photograph courtesy of Duke University Manuscript Department

The present Post Office Building was opened in March, 1934. Jim Farley was postmaster the day the new building began service. On that day, he received a check for the purchase of tobacco revenue stamps equal in amount to the entire cost of the new building. The photograph dates to 1939.

Photograph by Wootten-Moulton Studios

The formal opening of the Durham-Chapel Hill Boulevard occurred in 1953. At the ribbon-cutting ceremony were, left to right: Governor Kerr Scott; Gordon Gray, president of the University of North Carolina; Hollis Edens, president of Duke University; and Robert B. House of the University of North Carolina. Many welcomed the straight new road, a great improvement over the 52 curves to be negotiated on the old Chapel Hill Road.

Photograph courtesy of Wyatt T. Dixon

The new Durham City Hall at 101 City Hall Plaza, formerly an extension of Holloway Street, was dedicated April 2, 1978.

Photograph by Frank A. Kostyu

General Carl R. Gray, Jr., gave the dedication address of the Veteran's Administration Hospital on April 19, 1953. The hospital had officially opened on Arpil 6. It had 120 beds and a professional staff of 24 full-time physicians, 65 residents and interns, and 154 nurses. The total number of employees was 600. Today, there are 66 physicians, 139 residents and interns, and 251 nurses. The total number of employees is now 1,444.

Photograph courtesy of Wyatt T. Dixon

The aerospace exhibit of the North Carolina Museum of Life and Science, chartered in 1946, is privately financed and one of only four such collections in the world. It contains many artifacts relating to space explorations, including a diorama of the Apollo 16 moon landing. Here are the only facilities in the nation designed to teach the blind about aerospace. The Research Triangle Institute has made significant biomedical research contributions to the space program. This museum mirrors Durham's enthusiasm for and involvement in the future of space exploration.

Photograph courtesy of Durham Chamber of Commerce

This City Hall at one time had been the high school. This photograph was taken in 1977, when the future of the building was uncertain, from the corner of Manning and Morris Streets.

Photograph by Frank A. Kostyu

Durham was not without racial turmoil in the sixties. Some 700 neatly dressed demonstrators were arrested on May 20, 1963, at a peaceful sit-in on the property of the Howard Johnson Restaurant, Chapel Hill Boulevard. Arresting officers were deputies E. P. Tilley and C. P. Fogelman.

Photograph by Charles H. Cooper, Herald-Sun

Mayor Wade L. Cavin, fifth from left, leads the 14-mile run on July 17, 1977, which kicked off "Durham First" week. No prizes and no competition drove the runners on in 100-degree heat in the track capital of the world; they were celebrating the beginning of a three-year campaign of civic pride and community image-building, under the auspices of the Chamber of Commerce.

Photograph by Jim Sparks, Herald-Sun

The Durham Day parade, heading west at the corner of East Main and Corcoran Streets on Thursday, November 3, 1977, commemorates the designation by the National Register of Historic Places of downtown Durham as a historic district. The first solely commercial district in the state to be placed on the National Register, Durham Historic District includes 27 fine buildings representative of early twentieth century American architecture. Among the notable structures are the Central Carolina Bank Building (also known as Hill Building), the Post Office, the Durham Auditorium, and St. Phillips Episcopal Church.

Photograph by Tony Rumple

Summer, 1975, at Muirhead Plaza, Durham, formerly known as Five Points. The tall building, left rear, was the Durham Hotel, formerly called the Washington Duke Hotel, which was torn down in December, 1975. The small park at the corner of Chapel Hill Street and East Main Street was once the site of the first public library and subsequently the Piedmont Building. The Belk Building, the light-colored building to the right of the Durham Drug Company, was torn down in 1977. The Trust Building with its arched windows, stands behind the Belk Building. The Hill Building is now occupied by the Central Carolina Bank (CCB) and offices.

Photograph by Terry Cantrell

This is how the Pine Street Church looked on January 26, 1978. During the pastorate of James A. Cannon, in 1948, the congregation moved its home to the corner of Lincoln and Massey Streets and changed its name to the Covenant United Presbyterian Church. The new church is a community center for civic activities and shares in sponsoring several outreach programs.

Photograph by Frank A. Kostyu

The old cornerstone, worn by the weather.

Photograph by Frank A. Kostyu

When Durham's citizens drove or walked by the Pine Street Church on January 27, 1978, this is what they saw.

Photograph by Frank A. Kostyu

On January 28, 1978, the corner of Roxboro and Poplar Streets, the site of the Pine Street Church two days earlier, had become a neatly manicured lot.

Photograph by Frank A. Kostyu

The series of pictures making this panorama shot was probably taken in the mid-1920's.

The Post Office and Trust Building are seen in the right foreground, while the Washington Duke Hotel looms as the tallest building in Durham. In the left foreground is the Seaboard Freight Depot, where a parking garage is now. In the left center background is the Liggett-Myers factory. The twin spires of the Duke Memorial United Methodist Church are at the far left.

Many of the railroad tracks have been covered to make room for parking. To the right of the depot and near a railroad car is a horse-drawn wagon.

Photograph courtesy of Duke University Manuscript Department

SKYLINES

In 1978, Durham consists of 40 square miles. In 1890 the town comprised one square mile; by 1925 it had expanded to 12.8 square miles, and as recently as 1937, Durham was only 13.25 square miles in area.

A glimpse of Durham from a 1910 postcard. Small cottage homes abound in the rapidly developing community. Several landmarks of the time dot the skyline—the Trust Building, the First Baptist Church on Mangum Street, Fire Station #1, and Trinity Methodist Church.

Postcard courtesy of Duke University Manuscript Department

On the left is the building housing the Mechanics and Farmers Bank and formerly the North Carolina Mutual Life Insurance Company; it has been designated a National Historic Landmark. The steeple is that of the First Baptist Church when it was on Mangum Street. On the right, looking east on Main Street, we first see the tower of the Union Station and farther east is the old county courthouse. The pictures making up this panoramic shot were probably taken in the 1920's.

Photograph courtesy of Duke University Manuscript Department

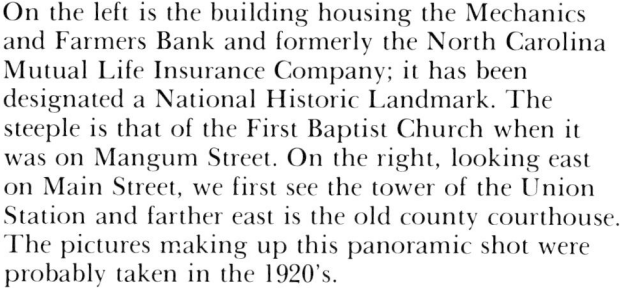

This panoramic photograph, looking east in the 1930's, shows how the railroad tracks and Union Station dominated Durham. To the far left can be seen Malbourne Hotel and First Presbyterian Church. Plainly visible are the old county courthouse, then Hotel Lochmoor; Union Station is in the center of the photograph. Off in the distant background are the smokestacks and watertowers of the textile factories. At the far right is the Steeple of Pine Street Presbyterian Church. Pine Street was renamed Roxboro Street on October 6, 1958, because it was a dominant continuation of that street.

Photograph courtesy of Duke University Archives

This photograph taken in the 1940's shows downtown Durham. In the center of the picture are Five Points and the Piedmont Building at the crossing of Main and Chapel Hill Streets. The Hill Building, erected in 1937, is the tallest building. Near it is the hotel originally known as the Washington Duke. At the end of Chapel Hill Street is the First Baptist Church. The Geer Building, now torn down, can be seen right of the Hill Building on Main Street. It was the former home of the Wachovia Bank. Across the street is the North Carolina National Bank Building, and below it is the Durham Hosiery Mill, that used to manufacture silk hosiery. The mill has since been razed. The American Tobacco Company can be seen across the railroad tracks on the right.

Photograph courtesy of State Department of Archives and History

Looking west along the railroad tracks from atop the North Carolina Mutual Life Insurance Building. In the foreground is Duke Memorial United Methodist Church, which fronts on West Chapel Hill Street. The East-West Expressway is at the extreme left, and the rear of the Liggett-Myers Tobacco Company, which fronts on West Main Street, is shown at right. The Dillon Supply Company on Duke Street is to the left of the Liggett-Myers building. Liggett-Myers tobacco warehouses can be seen in the center of the 1977 photo.

Photograph by Frank A. Kostyu

The view south from the North Carolina Mutual Life Insurance Building in 1977. The Alexander Ford Motor Company covers a large area. The American Tobacco Company and some of its warehouses dominate the center of the photograph. The East-West Expressway passes near the American Tobacco Company.

Photograph by Frank A. Kostyu

Looking west on West Chapel Hill Street. The Temple Baptist Church is at the left, with the Immaculate Conception Catholic Church across the street. The tower of Duke Chapel challenges the skyline in the distance. The picture was taken in 1977 atop the North Carolina Mutual Life Insurance Building.

Photograph by Frank A. Kostyu

Bird's eye view of Durham looking west. The tall buildings in the center are the Hill Building and the Durham Hotel. Up Chapel Hill Street is the North Carolina Mutual Life Insurance Building. The chapel of Duke University is barely visible at the center top of the photograph. The picture was taken prior to December, 1975, when the hotel was imploded.

Photograph courtesy of Durham Chamber of Commerce

Downtown Durham looking northeast from atop the North Carolina Mutual Life Insurance Building. The photo, taken in November, 1977, reflects the changes taking place.

Photograph by Frank A. Kostyu

ACKNOWLEDGMENTS

Numerous individuals and organizations have contributed to the birth of this book. We would especially like to extend our appreciation to the many citizens of Durham who shared with us their photographs, historical mementos, and anecdotes to enliven the historical record.

The authors found it a rewarding experience to work with Wyatt T. Dixon, who wrote a brief historical survey for this book. Through his long association with Durham both as a noted citizen and for many years as city editor of the *Durham Sun*, Wyatt has become an encyclopedia of facts about Durham. One of the pleasurable sidelights in preparing this book was to go to his quiet retreat in the countryside, where he was willing to recall significant information and events.

Those reading this book will find the reminiscences of Elsie W. Perkins (a pseudonym) a joy to peruse. The old timers will be touched by nostalgia; the young will be enlightened by what has been, what is, and what is yet to be.

For their enthusiastic interest and helpful suggestions, we would also like to thank: Stephen E. Massengill of the Division of Archives and History in Raleigh; William King and Mark Stauter of the Duke University Archives; Mattie Russell and Paul Chestnut of the Duke University Manuscript Department; Murray J. Marvin, senior vice president for corporate planning and communications of the North Carolina Mutual Life Insurance Company.

In addition, James R. McPherson and Mildred Harris of the Duke Homestead Tobacco Museum, Margaret Nygard of the Eno River Association, Jerry Gentry of the Durham Chamber of Commerce, the Blackwell Brogden family, Mr. and Mrs. George C. Pyne, Jr., Lee F. Ribet, and George Lougee gave information and/or pictures that contributed significantly to this book. Steven Stolpen supplied several photographs that he obtained through his research on Raleigh and Chapel Hill. John B. Flowers, III, offered valuable suggestions and materials and read the manuscript.

A photographic book involves, among other things, working in the dark. We want to thank Paul E. Kostyu for the many hours he spent helping us process film and the printing of over 300 photographs. Some of these old photographs required painstaking effort and patience, for which we are most grateful.

A final thanks goes to Marjorie Butcher Kostyu and Donna Dodd Kostyu, our wives, who significantly contributed their typing and editorial skills to this book, their thoughtful advice, and, most of all, their good-natured patience.

Several books and publications should be mentioned as valuable sources of information for those who want to know more about the roots of Durham: *The Story of Durham, City of the New South* by William K. Boyd (1925), *Black Business in the New South: A Social History of the North Carolina Mutual Life Insurance Company* by Walter B. Weare (1973), *The North Carolina Mutual Story* by William J. Kennedy (1970), *Bull Durham and Beyond* by John B. Flowers, III, and Marguerite Schumann (1976), *The Dukes of Durham, 1865-1929* by Robert F. Durden (1975), *Durham and Her People* by W. C. Dula (1951), and *The Cameron Plantation in Centrdl North Carolina (1776-1973) and its Founder Richard Bennehan* by Charles R. Sanders (1974).

A view of Durham's skyline through the windows of the Pine Street Church, which was razed at the end of January, 1978, reflects the spirit of change in Durham.

With nostalgia, citizens look back as history was made. With anticipation, Durham looks forward to making history.

Photograph by Frank A. Kostyu